Super Sparkly Everything

How connecting to God & personal responsibility
brought my life from struggle to sparkle.

Maria Milagros Vazquez

ISBN: 0-9993030-0-7
ISBN-13: 978-0-9993030-0-9

Jen.
you are extraordinary, and have nothing to prove. you are deserving and capable of every good thing. cultivating that - one step at a time. Deep breaths.
Mariah.

DEDICATION

This book is dedicated with all of my heart to the most amazing human I've ever known, my daughter Naima. You are incredibly positive and ridiculously resilient. You are my life's greatest gift and greatest teacher. You have permission to love yourself, evolve, change your mind, fight for your dreams, and live a super sparkly everything life.

You deserve it.

Con todo mi corazón, Mom

TABLE OF CONTENTS

Maria Milagros Vazquez

Chapter 1

ALLOW ME TO CLARIFY

Nothing can dim the light which shines from within. ~*Maya Angelou*

Welcome to *Super Sparkly Everything*. This is a book that has been living in my heart and my head for way too long. I decided to finally write it when I felt ready to share not just my principles, but also my stories, regardless of the feedback that I might get in response. I use the word feedback to describe both praise and criticism, and I do so with the utmost respect. What I need you to understand is that I am finally sharing this book because I know that it will be useful for many people who are stuck and are looking to live a greater, healthier, happier, authentic, truthful, more fulfilled, more grateful, more love filled life.

That being said, there are two disclaimers and an explanation that I want to put out there there right from the beginning.

Disclaimer 1: Some of these stories involve other people. No names are listed. All of these stories are as I remember them and from my perspective. If you recognize that you are in the story, please know that I share the story as a method of helping others and not to offend you. They are my memories from a very specific time in my life and at a specific age. They are a part of my truth and I recognize that my truth may not be yours.

Disclaimer 2: I am a child of the most high God. I discovered God as a child when I was physically broken. I accepted Him into my heart and my life while visiting someone in prison in my early 20's. I was emotionally and mentally broken at that time. I pursued a relationship with Him later into my 20's when I recognized that all of my emotional and mental brokenness, all of my depression and my battles, stemmed from being spiritually broken and disconnected. God and Jesus are real to me. No one can ever take away my experiences and encounters. That being said, I also recognize that not everyone calls their higher power God or Jesus. I want to be clear that this book is all inclusive. God has taught me that I have no place to judge or condemn others. My only job is to love. So please know that if you call your higher power something other than God or Jesus, I still had you in mind when I wrote this book. I believe that everyone has the right and deserves to live the super sparkly life that we were all promised. Within these pages I'm going to refer to the ultimate source, the master of the universe and the highest power as God. For each chapter you will find seven related scriptures in Chapter 14: Extras and References.

I wrote this book from a place of love and gratitude. I love my God and the gifts He has given me. I have realized that these stories and lessons are not my own and are meant to be used to lead the way for others. He has also given me the courage to write this book. I am assured that it will help at least one person, and in doing so, it will fulfill it's purpose. I am grateful that you decided to pick it up and give it a chance. I am excited about the very idea that super sparkly everything is for everyone and can be accomplished if you so choose to do the work.

Allow me to take a moment here and define what super sparkly everything means to me. I need to be clear about this. Yes, I'm a grown woman who says things like 'super sparkly everything'. Please do not confuse that with naivety. When writing this book, I made sure to include some of the stories from my past that will help you understand that my life was not always rainbows, unicorns, sunshine, kittens and glitter. However, I choose to create a different life than the one that I grew up in. The life that I'm worthy of. The life that I've been promised. The life that is my birthright. That life is super sparkly everything.

Let me break it down for you. When you first read *Super Sparkly Everything* you probably think about glitter and sequins being everywhere, and in some respects it is like that. When my daughter does a craft project with glitter it ends up everywhere. It is so hard to clean. It gets into the crevices of my hardwood floors. It mysteriously appears on our food. It always ends up in my hair, even if I am nowhere near her, the glitter, or the room where she is creating her masterpiece. I can sweep three times and swiffer once for good measure, but surely I will still find it for the next week or even month. Why do I seem to notice it everywhere? Because it catches and reflects the light. I can find it in the wood floor spaces when the sun peeks through the window or when the light comes on. It does what it is designed to do. It sparkles so that it can be seen. It is designed to add that little (or big) something extra to the craft project or art work.

Are you with me so far? Imagine a life where the sparkle that is in you, that has been designed and created, on purpose, to catch and reflect light, is allowed to shine. Imagine the greatness and the possibilities that your sparkle can add to your life's projects and your legacy, or your masterpiece. Imagine that it gets into the crevices of your life and the lives of those around you. It's sparkly and it's everywhere.

Let's take it one step further. Imagine a life where the *super* represents a supernatural connection. It represents direct and divine access to the ultimate life and light source. God. Imagine a life where the *sparkly* represents abundance. I use the word abundance but what I am referring to is so much bigger than that it is actually indescribable. It's not just the good stuff, it's the best and most desirable of the good stuff. It's living a life in peace, and in joy, and in gratitude, and in love. It's living a life with those things and all of their amazing byproducts. Imagine living a life where *everything* really means everything. It is sprinkled into every area of your life because where you are, there you are. Where you are, so is your sparkle. The sparkle is the thing that makes you special and unique. It adds that something extra. Everywhere you go you are there and so you bring the super sparkly living with you. Then, it is in your job, it is in your family, it is in your friendships, it is in your wallet, it is on your vacation, it is in your time, it is in your prayer life, it is in your body, it is in your food, it is everywhere. It is *everything.*

I have discovered that it is possible. It's not perfect by any means but it is possible. I am not perfect, don't pretend to be and honestly don't really know what that would even look like. I can tell you with honesty though that for the most part, I live this life. My goal is to help you find your freedom so that you can live this life as well. You deserve it. Do you know why? Because you are a child of the most high and it is your birthright.

You are blessed and a blessing. Enjoy!

Chapter 2

TIME TO MAKE A DECISION

It's not where you come from; it's where you're going that counts. ~*Ella Fitzgerald*

As a society we are becoming more and more dependent on medications, drugs and/or alcohol as a way of covering, smothering, or minimizing what is happening or has happened in our lives. I am meeting more and more people who are going through the motions of their everyday lives, waiting for something magical or miraculous to 'save' them. In the meantime, they are killing time and their feelings with the use of medications and/or drugs/alcohol. According to a study that was published in the Journal of the American Medical Association, 60-70% of Americans are on at least one prescription drug and more than half receive at least two prescriptions. Medical and Research Center, The Mayo Clinic, reports that antibiotics, antidepressants and painkiller opioids are the most common prescriptions given to Americans. Generally speaking, women and older adults receive the most prescription antidepressants. Opioids are being the most common among young and middle-aged adults.

Due to the continued increase in the amount of prescriptions being written for antibiotics, antidepressants and opioids, experts predict these prescriptions will soon become widespread among children as well. We are teaching our children to smother their pain and issues, and/or they are learning by the adult examples that are around them. This is a scary reality in our society but it doesn't have to be. There is a better way.

There is an actual way to live life to the fullest and not just exist and survive. There are actual ways to rescue ourselves and start living the kind of lives we were created to live. I imagine if you picked up this book you are a lot like me. You probably don't want to, or are tired of, smothering your feelings, whether they are bad or good. Certainly, you don't want to live like a zombie. I especially don't want my magnificent daughter who laughs every day and has so much to give to exist the way so many in society do today. I deserve more, she deserves more and you deserve more. We deserve to live a life that is super sparkly everything!

****

I am a Hispanic female who grew up in a drug infested and impoverished neighborhood. I suffered sexual abuse along with other abuses. Statistically speaking, I should be either in prison, on drugs, a combination of, or dead. That is what the statistics say about me based on my past facts. Unfortunately, I am sad to report that the stats were correct for many of my relatives and friends. At the same time, I am very happy to report that neither of those things are true for me.

My mother was a single mother of 6 children. There was usually a stepfather of sorts in the house for most of my youth, but please understand that being a warm body in a room is not the same as being a parent. During that time, it was clear to me that their role was to be with my mother, not to play the role of father to her children, even if some of those children were their own. From what my mother has told me, and my memory has chosen to repress, my own father was an abusive, drug addicted, alcoholic criminal. His fists found their way to her flesh constantly. One day when he took a standard and expected trip to jail, she escaped to another part of New York to start over. I spent the majority of my youth in the Bronx, hating myself and my body, abused by many 'trusted' people. I watched many succumb to the enticing life of drug use, a perfect escape from the woes of their realities. I did not care for the way their eyes looked glazed over, or how the apology always followed the excuse of "I was drunk", or "I was high."

Not wanting to escape in the conventional ways of the time, I instead became depressed and often entertained suicidal ideations. During this time the greatest release was dance. It was the one thing in my life that I could depend on, that made me feel alive and connected to something greater than myself. Dance gave me hope, and with the help of my dance teacher I even had the audacity to entertain the occasional thought that there was a better life awaiting me in the future. I tucked that thought far in the back of my mind, trying to protect its naivety, afraid that someone stronger or who knew better would take it from me, like they did my other innocences.

After watching a fellow neighborhood child die in a spray of bullets during a drug territory battle, my mother decided that she needed to move her children out of the Bronx in order to protect their survival. That gun fight happened on Thanksgiving. By December 9th, we were living with my old school, Puerto Rican grandparents. In that one act of diligence my mother unknowingly taught me that when something needs to get done for safety and health reasons, just get it done.

Moving to Massachusetts proved to be a social challenge. Being Puerto Rican in a predominately African American neighborhood of the Bronx meant you were just lighter than everyone else, that your mom cooked delicious rice and beans and that you would listen to fast and fun music also known as merengue and salsa. In Massachusetts, my Puerto-Rican-ness was constantly questioned by other Hispanics who didn't understand why I didn't wear eyeliner or have a boyfriend, why I didn't straighten my hair, why I dressed in baggy clothes, why I knew every word to the latest hip-hop songs, or why I didn't speak Spanish. It was a time of rediscovering who I was and how I was going to fit in, if at all. It was also a time of watching family members partake in obvious marijuana and cocaine use. It happened right there in my face because I was an 'invisible dumb girl', or too young to know what was happening, or something like that. And alcohol was everywhere, all the time for every and any reason.

Massachusetts was also the place where I really learned to grow up because my mother spent most of my high school years chasing after her man, in another country. After I moved out and went to college I realized that I was still suffering from depression, suffering from not knowing who I was, and suffering from toxic and unhealthy relationships in my life. Every time I thought I was making a change or getting ahead, life or the people in it just kept pulling me back. I was miserable and desperate and stuck.

Today I say things like, "Happy Monday!", and I mean it wholeheartedly. When I go places some people very sarcastically say things like "Here comes the sunshine." My absolute favorite way to sign off a text, email or letter is 'super sparkly everything'. And I write it because I mean it. It took me many years later to learn that my lack of self-love, not having any real standards or healthy rituals, was pulling me back and keeping me down. I eventually developed some principles that I decide to live by. I decide, every morning, to live by these principles and the rituals and standards that they entail. I don't always feel like doing it but I remember where I can end up, mentally, emotionally, physically and spiritually if I don't do these things. That possibility turns my 'maybes' into mandates. That is where I find my talents and strengths, take back the power and control of my life and live in the freedom that is intended for me.

****

In this book I will be teaching you the principles that you need to know in order to live a super sparkly everything kind of life. Every time I see those words, they make me smile. I think about where it came from.

One day I was sharing with my daughter an interaction that I had at work where a co-worker actually told me that I annoy her with my sparklyness. I had never heard someone refer to it as sparklyness, and I liked it. I appreciated her honesty and told her that. I also told her that I wouldn't stop being me to make her feel more comfortable. Before I walked away I wished her a 'super sparkly evening'. She rolled her eyes, chuckled and walked away. My daughter and I laughed at that sign-off and how ridiculous it sounded. But, it stuck with me.

Then, on a weekend getaway with some family, high in the mountains of Vermont, we decided to step outside and brave the cold to see what the sky looked like at night from that height. As our eyes found the sky we dropped our words and forgot about whatever statements we were making and stood, scattered on that mountain top, in awe of the galaxies and majesty that was right there. What I saw was nothing that I could have ever imagined outside of a planetarium. It was absolutely gorgeous. The crisp navy blue sky was illuminated with thousands upon thousands of stars, as far as the eye could see, in any direction. I had simultaneous feelings of being so small and of being so infinite. I was equal parts delighted that I had the privilege of seeing this greatness and sad that this is not the sky I see every night. I chose to remain present in that place and focus on the beauty that laid before me at that moment. No one spoke. No one could. We just stared. I looked around slowly and blinked intentionally, as if taking photos for my spirit to hold onto and review from time to time. Suddenly, I felt a small warm hand in my hand and looked down to see my daughter's face, illuminated from both the light of the stars and the light from her spirit. We smiled at each other and as she turned her gaze back to the sky she said "Super sparkly everything."

Yes indeed. Super sparkly everything is that place where we live in gratitude, in the present, and in love. It is a place where things aren't always great and almost never perfect, but they are always amazing and peace is never far away. It is that location, within us, where we take responsibility for ourselves and our lives and create action accordingly. Super sparkly everything is where we live in our truth, of our smallness and our greatness. It is a reminder that perspective is everything and that can be changed. It is internal joy in knowing that we are loved, so deeply and unconditionally by our creator. God, the heavenly father, who created the beautiful stars of the heavens also created us and we are also beautiful stars, who walk the earth. It is that place where we trust that He wants us to live our lives in abundance and to the full in every area of our life. That is super sparkly everything.

****

Here is the thing about super sparkly everything: everyone can get it and everyone deserves it. You deserve it. It is possible to live a happy, whole and fulfilled life regardless of where you are at this moment. It is possible regardless of where you come from or what you've been told. I know this because it is possible for me, and you and I are not that different. I am not an exception to any rule, at all. I have learned, the hard way, through a lot of trial and error, therapy and even medication, that there is a better way to live. There is! I want to share what I've learned and the steps that I have taken. Some of these will work for you, some you will tweak and some won't work at all. You have to start in order to figure it out. Part of the fun is in the figuring it out because you will be getting to know yourself better, and in doing that you will *be* better and *do* better. You can have it, one step at a time. You deserve it!

Over the years I realized that there are some basic principles that I now live by and teach. My goal, even throughout my jobs, has been and will continue to be to teach others these principles so that they don't have to go through as much as I did. I want them to get to the place of super sparkly everything as quickly as possible. We can either learn by example or learn by experience. This book is a combination of both. I will show you the example and you can decide whether you want to incorporate these steps into your life (experience).

When we are living in a place of unconditional love, with an attitude of gratitude, not taking ourselves or our lives so seriously and taking care of ourselves by being responsible for our lives, we are not just creating a better life for ourselves but for all that we come in contact with. We become better friends, siblings, spouses, parents, children, employees, employers, etc.

My experiences have demonstrated that when the people that I work with, from children to adults, implement these principles and steps into their everyday lives, they become happier and more fulfilled. The change is internal at first and then their external worlds reflect that. We were put here, filled with gifts and talents, light and hope, to love and care for one another. And, if we have been alive long enough we know that our relationships are the most important thing in life. The most important relationships are those that we have with our higher power and with ourselves. These relationships create the framework for all other relationships. We deserve to live in such a way that every person we come in contact with, whether for 5 minutes at the market or for 50 years in marriage, will be forever affected by the gifts and talents, light and hope and love that lives in us.

As stated earlier, in this book I am going to teach you the principles that will contribute to making your everyday life full of super sparkly everything. I am not just going to tell you about what they are. I will also provide you with practical steps to make it real. I have read a lot of books, listened to a lot of talks and attended a lot of sermons that were meant to help me in some area but lacked practicality. Although I was inspired and motivated in those instances, I found myself asking one of these three questions:

1. What does that mean?
2. How do I do that?
3. Where do I start?

So, my goal here is to help you answer those questions. I am going to give you the principles and then provide you with practical information, as well as steps, to help you understand and implement the principles. At the end of the book there is even a reference section with some videos, books, movies and music that keeps me and others in that super sparkly place. There is one catch though....I can't do the work for you. I already did the work for me and wrote the book for you. Now, it's your turn.

Do this for yourself. Do this for everyone you care about. Do it for the people you haven't even met yet but who will have the privilege to meet you. Do it because you are here to make a difference and that could be as simple as showing up as yourself and inspiring someone to do the same. You deserve a life that is super sparkly everything.

Chapter 3

THE WHY

Either I will find a way or I will create a way but I will not create an excuse.
~anonymous

Do you find that most people you talk to are always complaining about something? Do you see people going through the motions of their daily lives, not having time to do the things that they want to do or really enjoy? Are you that person? Some of us are taught by our well-intended families, friends and medical professionals that life happens *to* us. We are taught that if we are off in some way, or if there is a 'chemical imbalance', the only way to deal with it is by medication. Today, more doctors are reaching for their prescription pads as a way to pad the common day to day issues people walk into their office with. As anyone who has ever been on medication to help lessen sadness or increase happiness can attest, for the most part it just kind of makes you numb.

I know that there are going to be a lot of critics who will say that many depressed people need the antidepressants to survive. To that, I would dare to say that the medication cannot be their ultimate source. People have within them the power and the capacity to pull out all of their gifts, talents and strengths that bring a sense of fulfillment and happiness. I would dare to say that when we learn to truly forgive and to operate from a place of love and gratitude, most people can create for themselves a life where the 'antidepressants' come from their new and healthy rituals and standards. The key to all of this already lives inside of every person. We have to take responsibility for our lives and begin to do things differently. We need to change our input so that we can change our output. The problem is that the medication companies want you to believe that you cannot live without them and that this mediocre existence is the best there is. That is a flat out lie. Studies have proven time and time again that we have the capacity to cure our own depressions by taking control of our lives, making solid decisions about what we will focus on, and taking action accordingly. It has been tested and shown that we can, by controlling our thoughts, words and actions, change our brain chemistry. We can alter the state of our minds and the structure of our brains without medication. Don't just take my word for it though. Look it up! Discover the truth for yourself.

Now, please do not misunderstand me. Gains in the medical world are great to help someone in a real and serious time of medical need. Medications can be a great support for someone who is experiencing a really difficult time. Becoming dependent on them and not having another plan in place to wean you off is what concerns me. People begin to find a sad semblance of something that may look like happiness and begin to believe that is the best it will be. Remaining a victim to their circumstances and identifying with their pain is the concerning part. I am also not saying that if you are currently on a medication you should throw them out. No, quite the opposite. You should do the research, figure out a healthy plan and course of action, and go see your doctor about implementing this new plan so that you can slowly and carefully come off of your antidepressants. That new plan may include exercise, overhauling your diet, and making conscious decisions to spend some time recognizing what you're thinking about and pushing yourself to make necessary and positive changes.

As for myself, I know that during my brief stint with medications I became increasingly sad. A close family member who was on medication had the experience of becoming completely indifferent, unable to care or feel in the same way he used to. Too many people are going through their minutes waiting for something to come along and fix them. They are melancholy and their lives are monotonous. They are bored, unfulfilled, depressed or traumatized.

We are spirit beings having a temporary physical experience here on this planet. This experience, this journey, is not meant to be clouded by the effects of medications. We are not meant to live in a daze or dependent on a substance, legal or not. Here is the thing we might not want to hear: Bad things have happened, are happening and will happen. We are, and are surrounded by, imperfect people who are acting in ways that fulfill a need or belief. As such, we will hurt, offend, disrespect and injure each other. That is going to happen. We seem to forget that part of the experience is going to include the negative emotions, sad feelings, anger, frustration etc. We get to experience all of them and then we get to choose where we stay and what we focus on. If we are paying attention, the negative or sad stuff is actually stretching us, pushing us, showing us that we have no limits and hopefully making us better people. We get to choose though. That is the whole thing, we get to choose. Staying stuck is not the way to live. No one wants to stay there.

Now, on the other hand, you know those people who walk into a room and rather than let the vibe of the room affect them, they arrive with the vibe and push it into the space. Some people are annoyed by their cheery disposition and glass-half-full conversations. Others are excited to be around them, in hopes to brush up against them, and catch something that they have or pick up indicators on how to be like that. What they are sensing is that person's positivity, love and gratitude. They have an ability, a learned skill, of focusing on what is good in life and work at keeping themselves in that place. Well, that is me. Hello.

Yes, you read that right. It is a learned skill and initially, it is work. This is great news because it means that it is possible for anyone. And, bonus, the work gets easier the more you do it. Eventually it isn't work anymore. What starts off like a type of chore for some, becomes second nature and then just becomes your nature. People will start saying "Well, that's just how she or he is." News flash: No one JUST IS any kind of way. They learned to be that way. At some point that learned behavior, whether negative or positive, served a purpose. Well, I'm here to let you know that through learning new positive techniques and rituals, and through consistent and disciplined action, you can begin to see your life change for the better.

Perhaps you'll even make up your own fun catch phrase to describe your life. It will just be you being you and loving yourself and your life. You will love life and love living. You will have that without having to drive the fanciest car, or wear all the brands, or whatever it is you previously believed you needed to make you happy. The beauty of this is that if you want the fancy car and the brands and the stuff, you can have those as well. So long as they don't come before the really important stuff and you recognize that they are not the things that make your life super sparkly everything.

The problem is that we are being inundated with information telling us that this is the only way to heal or help anything and everything that we are dealing with. You have probably seen one of these commercials where there are people frolicking through the meadows as the narrator describes how wonderful your life will be on the medication. He does that right before he lists all of the serious and dangerous side effects to the medication. I know many people who while on these medications are in need of other medications to curb the side effects of the first one. And each medication comes with it's own side effects as well.

Times are changing. We are able to use medical breakthroughs to create cures and heal diseases and illnesses that have been hindering people for so long. Most people are getting caught up in the beliefs about medications as a cure all and surrendering their own powers and the power of God to move in their lives. They are allowing themselves to become victims to their circumstances rather than victors over their circumstances. We were designed to enjoy every area of our lives and we can't do that, for better or worse, if we don't take responsibility for our lives and every aspect of it. Clearly the current way isn't working. People are refilling their prescriptions but are not refining their perspectives or thoughts. People are miserable and that is a crying shame. When a person is miserable they aren't tapping into their gifts, promoting a healthy lifestyle or healthy choices, and are stuck. They are looking for someone to teach them how to break old patterns and take the steps to being and doing better. If I am hitting a nerve because I am talking to you about feeling stuck and needing fulfillment, with or without the medication aspects, then please take a real hard look at yourself. Is this life working for you? Are you sick and tired of being sick and tired? Are you ready to become the person who brings the good vibes? Are you ready for a super sparkly everything kind of life?

That is why I had to write this book. After my daughter was born I suffered from postpartum depression and a slight case of paranoia. When I realized that I spent more days crying and fighting dreadful thoughts, I finally caved and went to see my new doctor. After a few minutes of questions and answers, she quickly turned to the drawer, grabbed her prescription pad and a pen and handed me a tiny sheet of paper with some scribbles on it. On the way out the door, she tapped me on the knee and said "Stick in there." I remember thinking "Are you kidding me?" I got down off the crumbled paper and feeling crumbled on the inside went down the hall to my previous doctor who did not accept my new insurance. I walked in and asked the front desk receptionist if I could squeeze in a quick chat with her and that I would pay out of pocket. She asked me to sit and wait while she checked in with the doctor. After a short time the doctor came out and greeted me as if we were old friends. Once in the room I told her what was happening and what had just happened. She looked at the prescription and deciphered the code. Her eyes widened and she said "Woah, that's a lot of drugs." We discussed the last time I was on an antidepressant (actually 3 different types to be more specific). Each made me feel worse than the previous. It was that go-around with medications that made me leave my previous doctor and led me to her. She was the first medical doctor that I met who believed that we have within us the capacity to alter our moods and pull ourselves from whatever state we are in. She taught me that what I needed was daily action not a daily pill.

She was very clear that there was an actual chemical imbalance because my body was making the transition from having carried and developed a baby to no longer having to do that work. She carefully explained that most women go through this because their is a significant hormonal shift happening. After some discussion I walked out of her office with a new piece of paper. It was a plan. It was a daily action plan that required consistency, discipline and patience. It involved every aspect of myself from my spirituality, to my thoughts, taking care of myself in terms of food, sleep and movement, to my relationships, to what I was reading and watching. It was a skeleton of a plan and I had to take the time to figure out what each of those meant to me and put meat on the bones.

Tired of feeling that way, I carried that paper around with me until every item had a task list. Once I began implementing them, I realized that just as before, when I was suffering from depression and there was no pill to 'fix' me, I had to do some work. Each day got a little easier than the one before. There were occasional set-backs or slip ups but for the most part I was moving forward and could feel myself getting better. Eventually, I was back to my regular self and life was all good again.

I share this story to let you know that I get it. I understand feeling stuck, I understand depression and I understand postpartum. All of those things that I did then are in this book. They are right here on these pages, waiting for you to put them into action so that you can start living your best life now. Whether you are on medication or not, there is a way to live so that you are living in the fullness of your life. Fully aware, fully alert, fully feeling, fully enjoying and fully loving.

A few clarifying points:

1.   I am in no way stating that anyone should throw their medications out and do this instead. If that is

the path that you and your doctor decide is right for you, you need to be properly weaned from those medications.

2. The doctor who wrote me the prescription was a MD (medical doctor). The doctor who helped me create the plan was a DO (doctor of osteopathic medicine). They regard the body as an integrated whole, rather than treating for specific symptoms only.

3. There are some severe mental health cases that require medication as the patient undergoes intensive therapy and treatment. Please continue to take those and do what you have to do for yourself and your health.

This book can help anyone who is willing to put in the time and energy to make these action steps a reality. There are 2 types of people and as I describe them below you can decide, with your wonderful free will and capable minds, what kind of people category you fall into.

Maybe People. Maybe People say maybe a lot. These are people who want to keep going about their day to day lives ignoring that burning desire to be truly happy and to live with love. They prefer to stay in that comfortable, albeit, sad and/or boring place. There is no work or challenge required there. Without the work and the challenges there is also no tapping into their greatness and finding fulfillment and sparkle. People who want to wake up every day complaining about a day that just started and go to bed with a list of reasons why their life still sucks, please return this book or give it away. No pressure and no judgement. Those people are not ready to leave their own pity party yet, even though the chips are stale, the balloons are deflated and the music is boring. Those people prefer to stay comfortable in their misery because at least they know what to expect. Maybe people are too comfortable to make a real decision at this time. They stay in the maybe.

Mandate People. Mandate People are people who are ready to wake up everyday feeling excited and energized about what God will do with and through them that day. They want to live in the present, enjoying their moments, their relationships and themselves, in a place of love and gratitude. People who want to go bed with a sense of accomplishment and fulfillment and sleep peacefully knowing that they showed up in all of their glory and wonder, and have contributed to the world. They will awake refreshed. They desire to make a contribution and move the world into a better place, pushing themselves to be and do better. Mandate people make it a priority in their lives to do and be their best and are ready to face it all head on.

Maybe people will read this book and may make some changes. *Mandate people* will read this book and start making the changes along the way. Who are you and what do you want? We are responsible for our own lives. If we are sitting around waiting for somebody to come along and save us, fix us or help us, we are wasting time. If there were a movie about your life, you should be the lead character. If there were a comic book about your life, you should be the hero. This is your one life and you can take back your power and control. You can make the changes you need to make in order to live your best, most authentic, fulfilled and fun life. God has given us everything that we need in order to be our greatest self. If you don't believe me, I'd like to invite you to please read your bible. 2 Peter 1: 3-4 from one of my message bibles says that 'everything that goes into a life of pleasing God has been miraculously given to us and we were also given absolutely terrific promises to pass on.' You see, other than yourself the only other force that can help you move forward in your life is God. That life that pleases God is a life of purpose and joy, gratitude and love, fulfillment and fun! It pleases Him when we are being the best versions of ourselves. In taking responsibility we have to do the work to develop our relationship with Him, discover all that we are, and all that we are called to be. In that relationship, in that safe place, we get to operate in our truth and in our gifts. When we do that and start impacting the world for the better and increasing the capacity of mankind to excel. Then, we begin to live in the super sparkly everything kind of life.

****

Here is my purpose. As a youth, before I even knew what my purpose was I did know that I wanted a better life. I've always had this greater force pulling me to do better and be better. I knew this, even as a child and even when life seemed really bad. I've always known that it could get better if I wanted it to. I've always had the ability to hear the whispers of God telling me that I deserve greatness because I am greatness. I didn't always know what that voice was and my life gave me plenty of reasons to ignore it. When I was younger I defined greatness as money and tangible things. I always thought that I would know when I had arrived by the size of my bank account and the things that surrounded me. As an adult I've realized that it's not about the stuff on the outside, it's about the stuff on the inside. I now define greatness as living in my truth, knowing that I am a child of the most high, and loving myself. I define my greatness as being the best version of myself, who I can be from moment to moment, knowing that I'm a work in progress. In doing that, I also give permission to my daughter to do the same.

Speaking of my superb daughter, she reminds me everyday that my life is not my own. She is a representative for every living human on the planet. You see, she is a reminder that everyone deserves to be loved and to live in their greatness. She represents every single human that is on their journey. She represents the reasons to be grateful in my life. She represents happiness and joy. Her life, and the fact that I was blessed with the privilege to take part in creating that life, represents miracles. Miracles are everywhere and happening all around us and within us. Miracles are in the fact that we walk the planet. Miracles are in the fact that we are these amazingly dynamic and complex people filled with greatness. So, doing God's work, and loving my daughter, are my combined life's purpose. Love for them, love for myself, and love for you, is my purpose. My purpose helps me realize that my story is not my own and it's meant to be shared. The why, my purpose and my driving force, is love. Captured in one word the driving force behind this book is love. Super sparkly everything love!

Chapter 4

FRESH START

Some people feel the rain. Others just get wet. ~Roger Miller

My mother recalls...As the rain began to quicken its race to the earth her breathing became sharpened. Her deliberate gasps for release grew in their desperation. The pain spread across her hips and pushed its way into her lower back. She quickly scanned the room but could not locate what she was looking for. Suddenly, she felt a surge of moisture saturate her tattered second hand summer dress. It was time. Mustering up the strength that she knew laid deep inside, she pushed herself up to her feet, grabbed the hand of her 2 year old son and headed into the downpour. Her bare feet splashed the puddles as they quickly powered along the concrete. Each splash made the boy laugh with excitement and young wonderment. His laughter seemed to increase the pain and the intentional deep breathing was no longer helping. No cars or people were around during the early morning with its dark sky like night. It was just this 17 year old expectant mother and her first born. Unable to continue and severely afraid that her second child would be born in the summer rain on that broken Staten Island street she began yelling out for help. No one answered back. Finally, the father of her children came driving up with a friend after another night of hanging out and drinking. His friend transported her little family to the closest hospital. It was a small hospital run by nuns and nurses. One nun visited the young mother shortly after the birth of her daughter, who was to be named Maria after both of her grandmothers, and stated that it was a miracle that this child wasn't born on the street. So, it was decided that her middle name would be Milagros, meaning miracle.

****

As a teenage girl she reluctantly handed the almost 30 year old man his daughter (me) and tried to pretend that she couldn't smell the liquor on his breath or see the fresh needle marks on his arm. She pretended to not notice for too many days to count. About a year and a half later, several dozen beatings, two hospital trips and one attempt to kill her son, she finally decided enough was enough. It was only a matter of time before he'd land himself back in jail and when he did, she'd make her escape. During her waiting time her prayers began to grow simpler, "God, please let him hit me and not the kids. And, if he does, please don't let me die." She recalls that the next time he went to jail and she escaped with her children, it was raining outside.

****

I share with you these pieces of my birth and early childhood so that you can be assured that life was not handed to me on a golden, sparkly, glitter covered platter. I share these pieces of my story here and throughout this book to remind you that you are not alone. Yet, no matter where you started or how, and no matter who your parents are or aren't, you can start over right now.

At the start of each chapter you will read another piece of my story. These stories were once the very things that I allowed to hold me back, to hinder me and to depress me. Then I decided that I wanted to live. I wanted to actually and presently live, not exist and go through the motions with everyone else, constantly complaining about the cards that I was dealt. I decided that it was time to learn how others, who had been given a similar hand or worse, strategically played each card in order to get themselves to the best place and ultimately start winning at the game of life. In playing full out I have accepted that the greatest competitor that I have to deal with is the me from yesterday. If I am constantly pushing myself to grow and then using that growth to help others do the same, then I am creating positive impacts in the world and I am winning.

I am not that different from you. Please know that you don't get to say that I was born with certain traits, abilities or blessings that make this super sparkly life easy for me. That's a lie and I am hoping that you are reading this book because you are tired of that lie. When you tell yourself that about me or any other person who is presently living their lives, you are just creating an excuse for why you aren't living in your greatness. You're minimizing your greatness as if theirs is the exception to the rule. Let's just agree that we've all had enough of that.

If you believe in God, or any power greater than yourself, then you must know that He gives blessings and favor to all without exception. What is available for me is also available for you. What I am capable of, you are capable of. It won't always look the same for everyone but it IS possible. The difference between those who have and those who don't, is a simple matter of those who do and those who don't. It will require doing the work that will allow you to be open and accepting of the blessings and the abundance. You have to love yourself, you have to know you are perfect. You have to know that you are deserving and worthy. You have to know what your gifts are and use them every day.

I wrote this book as a reminder of these really important and key things and to teach you how to live a super sparkly everything life because you deserve it. Because the people around you deserve it. Because, if you are a parent, your children deserve it. Because the world needs you to live and operate in your greatness. That is the super sparkly everything.

Every time it rains, even in the cold of winter, when I know the water will form dangerous ice on the paths and roads, I find myself pausing just to have a listen. With every new rain I feel overwhelmed with the sensation of rebirth. It is as if the rain, with all of its power from the heavens, is able to wash away any past hurts or sins. This miraculous water from the sky is able to move down my flesh and capture the dirt that clings to my soul. Tiny dew drops capture my pain or shame and carry it past my feet, onto the ground and down the gutter, where it belongs. I feel this happening even when I am removed from the rain. On that special occasion when I take my daughter into the spring or summer warmth to play and splash and kick puddles, I can literally feel the cleansing. The scent of rain, like newness, lasts on and in me. These are God's cleansing showers and reminders that we can start over anytime. A rainy day feels more like a rebirth than any new year's or birthday. Super sparkly everything, larger than words, captured in every small rain drop.

****

People who know me now are always so surprised when they hear about pieces of my story from my childhood and early adulthood. They are surprised to hear about how much I had to learn, unlearn or relearn throughout the years in order to get myself to the place I currently am. When they ask me for the 'secret' to my positivity I always chuckle a little before I tell them that it is not a secret. It is not etched on a stone in a hidden cavern somewhere far, far away. Nope. It is in our faces every day and it is begging to be acknowledged. It was disciplined work. It was work, every single morning, whether I wanted to or not, until it became my new way of living. Every morning just like I had to choose to get out of bed and brush my teeth, I had to choose to focus on what was good, positive, lovely and all that I had to be grateful for. It's not a secret at all. It is the very thing that a lot of people would rather avoid and stay stuck.

If someone would have told me 20 years ago that my catch phrase at this time in my life would be 'super sparkly everything' I would have definitely warned said person that there was probably a large dose of ammonia in their batch of crack. No, really, I would have referred to crack. Bear with me, I grew up in the Bronx during a time when crack was all the rage and that is where my subconscious goes. I hear someone say something crazy and I think, you clearly smoke crack. So here is where someone who knew me from back in the day would ask *how did that girl, who grew up in the Bronx, surrounded by drugs and all that entails, end up becoming a woman who says things like super sparkly everything?* Let me explain.

In the next chapter you are going to get a glimpse of the seven main principles that I live by to achieve the super sparkly everything life. Chapters 6-12 are going to take a deeper dive into each principle and give you some actual how-to steps so that you can begin incorporating action into your everyday lives. By following the steps your life will begin to alter as you create new rituals and standards for yourself. Each of these chapters will begin with another story from my past that was not so sparkly. Again, I share these stories as a way of reminding you that you are not alone in your struggles and in your pain. I had to come to the conclusion that I deserve a better life and I that I wanted it more than I wanted to stay stuck and miserable. I had to come to the reality that the only person who can save me was me. I had to come to the decision to take action and be the lead and the hero of my story. I had to decide to start taking action. I hope you do as well.

Chapter 5

LUCKY NUMBER 7

First, it is an intention. Then a behavior. Then a habit. Then a practice. Then a second nature. Then it is simply who you are. ~Brendon Burchard

When I was younger I remember reading somewhere that the number 7 is the number of completion and the number of perfection. I really liked the sound of that and decided that 7 would be my favorite number. For example: there are seven days in the week so when the week is over, it is complete. God created the earth in seven days and it was perfect. When I decided to write this book I had notes galore. I organized my beliefs and ideas about super sparkly everything into categories and as it would turn out there are 7 main categories. Each of these then became a principle. These are the principles that I live by and teach. I can testify that I am healthy, happy, grateful and positive. Those who have created positive change in their lives using these steps have reported feeling whole, healthy and joyful.

The principles are:

1. **Put God first.** *(Chapter 6)* When we put God first, in all we do, we are establishing the proper order for living. We love because HE loved us first. In developing this relationship we are also opening ourselves to be constantly reminded of who we are, whose we are, and how we are meant to live. It is also in that relationship that we will always have safe harbor and a place to lay our burdens down. When we spend time with someone and learn to trust them we also believe that they are going to be there for us when we need them. Well, God is always there, always safe and will always take care of us. With Him is also a place where you can be raw and honest without condemnation.

2. **Love yourself.** *(Chapter 7)* God tells us that we must love our neighbor AS we love ourselves. This indicates that there is a demand on us to love ourselves after we love Him. The proper order is to love God and then love ourselves. In our society we are not generally told or taught to love ourselves. We are constantly told what the standard of beauty is, that we are not smart enough or good enough and that we need to struggle to attain perfection in order to be loved or accepted. That is a lie! God tells us that we are masterfully made. When we love ourselves and prove that with action, time and energy, we are better in every way and every area of our life benefits. When we truly and unconditionally love ourselves we are no longer afraid of rejection because we know in our hearts that the only one we need approval from is God. We then start to make healthier choices for ourselves and find that we are happier. When we allow ourselves to fully accept and love ourselves as we are, we can also begin to complement and contribute. We spend so much time competing and complaining. Usually when we do that it again comes from a place of fear. There is a fear of

not being enough or not ever being able to be enough. We tend to forget that we are perfect in God's eyes and that His blessings are infinite. Well, allow me to remind you that He is the same today, tomorrow and forever. See Principle #1. He will never leave us or forsake us and His abundance is limitless. We learn that we don't need anyone else's approval because we are loved and approved by God. We then accept that love and fully embrace it knowing that we cannot be anyone else and they cannot be us. We are all uniquely beautiful and perfect.

3. **Conquer your thoughts**. *(Chapter 8)* Our minds are extraordinary machines with programs and a ridiculous amount of information. It recalls things from our far away or recent past and creates programs that we then operate from. We could be minding our own business and washing dishes when suddenly the mind pulls up a thought about something that happened to you that makes you feel bad about yourself. Where did that come from? Why is it haunting me? The bible states that as a man thinketh, that he is. The bible has been telling us for 2000 years what scientists are discovering in this century and that is that our thoughts control our reality. So, when we learn to control our thoughts we learn to control the course, direction and mood of our lives. Please keep in mind that happiness is a choice. So, please choose it. As touched upon in the previous principle, thoughts control mood. We can control our thoughts and thereby can control our mood. Happiness is a mood, so we can choose to let it in or keep it out. There is work required here and the choice is ultimately ours. This does not mean that we should be fake or put on a smile after we suffered a loss. Every feeling was meant to be felt and processed. Even Jesus experienced anger. He reminds us though not to go to bed angry and that the fullness of joy is ours. He tells us that the morning brings joy. We can

feel every feeling. If it is a negative feeling we should allow ourselves the proper time to process and/or mourn/grieve and then begin to establish a plan for getting ourselves back to the place that God intended for us, happiness.

This includes having an attitude of gratitude. When we live our lives and operate from a place of gratitude we increase our ability to be present and to be happy. Embracing this way of living also has great effects on how we perceive our lives and the events or situations that happen in it. Regardless of how bad things seem or appear we are able to maintain our gratitude and find good in all things. I did some research and read every book I could get my hands on; secular, scientific and spiritual, to try and understand the power of gratitude and why an attitude of gratitude is the way that God wants us to live. Turns out, gratitude is transformative- for the mind, body, and spirit.

4. **Protect your temple.** *(Chapter 9)* We must take the time to take care of our bodies and the temple that we live in. When we fuel our bodies with the proper foods and we get appropriate amounts of movement, which the body was designed to do, we feel better and then do better. When we do that, we find ourselves feeling energetic, strong, and capable. Taking care of our bodies with healthy eating and active living also contributes to stronger immune systems, decreased chance of getting depressed, increased ability to combat stress and ability to sustain everyday activities. When you take the first letter of each of the words from Healthy Eating Active Living, you get the word HEAL. Coincidence? I think not. We can literally heal our bodies and our minds when we attend to them in healthy and appropriate ways. We just have to take the time to actually figure out what works for us. We start by making small changes and then allowing those changes to eventually become our new lifestyle. God gave us these amazing

bodies as a vessel to do the work that He has called us to. Taking care of our bodies is a form of worship and gratitude. When our temples are healthy, so are we and then we can continue to create, with energy, the super sparkly everything life that we desire and deserve.

5. **Life is a journey.** *(Chapter 10)* We must remember that everyone, including ourselves, is on a journey. When we approach people and ourselves while holding this thought in the forefront of our minds we are more likely to keep patience and compassion there as well. Not everyone is at the same place in life. Nor are all people able to handle stress the same way. Remembering this allows us to be more understanding of someone's current situation and reactions. It also helps to keep us from taking things personal. When we can do that we can also show up ready to give what we have to help others along on their journeys. When we do that, the outcome is powerful because we are contributing as intended. As with any journey, the goal is to keep moving forward along our paths and trusting that God will make them straight. We get to make stops to recharge and refuel. We get to make friends and pick up travel companions along the way. We get to have fun and celebrate. We get to help others and make an impact. We get to change courses sometimes. There will be detours and stops that take longer than they should. The key is to enjoy the journey and to be patient with ourselves along the way.

6. **Know who you're with.** *(Chapter 11)* When we start to make changes in our lives for the better it is of major importance that we are aware of who we are surrounding ourselves with. Our relationships are the most important things in our lives, and people who don't have real and intimate relationships suffer a great void. We are not designed to live in isolation. This is both beautiful and scary

because we tend to attract and connect with, whether we realize it or not, the kind of people that we are. If we are gossipers we will find that we align ourselves with and attract people who gossip. If we are positive and cheerful then we find it difficult to spend a lot of time around negative and cynical people. It is exhausting because it is not in alignment with who we are or who we want to be. The bible tells us that we must choose our friends wisely because those relationships impact our behaviors, and who we become. In this chapter we are going to take a deep dive into the questions that will help you decide if the relationships that you currently have align with self-love and your future goals.

7. **You're the hero.** *(Chapter 12)* Yes. You read that correctly. We have to take responsibility for every area of our lives, like the hero does. Step in and take charge. We get to put on our super suit of love, our cape of gratitude and take charge of our lives. We can't fly as high, or at all, if we are weighed down by the force of unforgivingness. The first step is to forgive and release anyone who came against us. Forgiving ourselves for any mistakes that we made and remembering that we will make more is also a part of the journey. For some this can come with a prayer and for others it will have to come with some professional help. Taking responsibility for our lives includes seeking that help if that is what we need. We do that by taking action in every way that we can. Getting off the couch and actually doing something about health. Eating better. Paying attention to relationships and releasing any that are negative or depleting is also a necessity. This also involves educating ourselves and deciding to invest in ourselves in order to get to where we want and need to be. The bible says that the people are destroyed for a lack of knowledge. It can be something as simple as finding out the difference between a DO and a

MD to decide the best type of doctor for our needs. It can also mean finding information about budgeting and finances. We learn that in loving ourselves we deserve to invest in ourselves. Buy a book, take a class, or as in my case, pay a late library fee. Educate yourself in the areas of your life where you are lacking and gather that knowledge. Educate yourself to get answers to questions you have. Educate yourself to learn more about things you enjoy doing. Educate yourself to develop your passion. We are either growing or dying and we might as well be growing. Of all the things that can be taken from us, education is not one of them. When we implement what we learn, it will not only better our lives but the lives of all those around us. Combining all that you have learned with all that you are will help you become the best superhero ever. Or should I say, the best super sparkly hero ever.

****

I just want to be clear in case you didn't pick up on my subtle cues, there is no secret sauce. There is no magic wand. There are no spells that we can cast. There is not going to be a delivery of a new life in a box at your door because you pressed a button online. What there will be: Work. Discomfort. Sacrifice. Inconvenience. Please allow me to explain before you drop this book in the recycling bin and run for your life. If you keep reading you may even get motivated to run towards actually living.

Work. If you want something in your life to change you have to be willing to do the work. I appreciate the way Tony Robbins words it, "If you want something you've never had, you have to be willing to do something you've never done." Whether you realize it or not, you have been working until now to create the life you are living right now. Ouch. When we repeat thoughts of worry and negative habits we create a life of worry and negativity. So now that we desire a life of peace and positivity, we have to get to the work of creating that life with our thoughts and habits. It is scary to know how simple it is. I wrote simple, not easy. You worked really hard to hold onto that life and you did well. Clearly, you are ready for the next level, so it is time to change course and do a different and new kind of work. Remember, what you input into your mind creates the output of your life.

Discomfort. The discomfort comes from challenging ourselves to be more and live better. Success happens outside of our comfort zone. Adventure happens outside of our comfort zone. The magic of presently living happens outside of our comfort zone. Joy and fulfillment happen outside of our comfort zone. So, it's time to get uncomfortable by getting out of your comfort zone. You picked up this book because in one way or another your comfort zone is not feeling so comfortable anymore. It might actually be getting on your nerves because somewhere deep down you know you want and deserve more. You have 2 choices now. You can stay there and find more reasons to complain and worry. Or, you can get out of there and create the life you really want.

Sacrifice. Most people see that word and they think about Jesus going to the cross for our sins. The sacrifice I'm talking about here will require us to die to our old way of thinking and living. It will require us to bury it and move on. The sacrifices will be about giving certain things up that we currently enjoy, or rather, that bring us temporary happiness in order to make room for the things that will benefit us in the long term and bring us permanent joy. For example, you might have to give up cigarettes in order to enjoy a healthier and longer life for yourself and your family. You might need to give up that television show that follows the day to day lives of those other people so that you can start creating and living the life you were designed to live. The kind of life that other people want to watch and learn from.

Fair warning: Sometimes it will get a little difficult. Just think, if that is real for your regular humdrum life, why wouldn't it be real for your great life? I don't know about you, but, I would much rather deal with unexpected challenges and difficulties while living a super sparkly everything life filled with love and gratitude than to have them while living a mediocre life. The reality is that when we start living a super sparkly life, it's not all that hard anymore. Our perspective changes and so does our outlook. We begin to view problems as opportunities and tend to focus on the good, even in the sad times. The life we deserve to live will require us to do some reading when we want to take another nap. It will require us to do the hard work of getting to know yourself and loving yourself, when we'd rather avoid the mirror. It will require consistent and disciplined action. That is not easy. That is not convenient.

Here's the best part though: It is all worth it! It is worth it because you will wake up every morning feeling energized, ready to take on your day. You will operate from gratitude and love every day and you will sleep knowing you lived in your truth, took responsibility, made an impact and loved. You are worth it!

****

As previously stated you are going to have some challenges. There are going to be daily challenges that may throw you off course. There will be situations and events that occur that require your time and energy and take you away from the other things that you want to be doing or should be doing. This is where scheduling comes in. Even if all we can block off to do this work is 10 minutes, it is a start and we have to start somewhere. There are going to be real resource limitations. This stuff is all real and is to be expected. When you start something like this with your mind already set that nothing will work out exactly according to your plan and trust that God will guide you and be there all the while, you are less likely to get discouraged or frustrated when these times inevitably arise. In working towards being super sparkly you will hopefully begin to perceive these challenges as something that is happening *for* you rather than just *to* you. You will begin to understand that there are lessons to be learned. You will strengthen your ability to find joy in all circumstances. Let us not get so caught up in making plans that we miss God's purpose. We have to be open and ready for whatever will come, because in that detour could be a great blessing or lesson that we need to get to where we want to go. We have to leave room for the the master of the universe to move.

      For some of you there will also be real resource limitations. Those resources are most likely going to be time, money, and mentors. As a single mother I had 2 great obstacles. Or at least they seemed like obstacles at the time. The first was time. I needed more time to do all of the things I had to do in a regular day. I worked, taught dance 1 night a week, my daughter had her extracurriculars and there was the regular day to day stuff like cooking, eating and cleaning that needed to get done. Add to that the required amount of daily time set aside to tend to my back and do all of the things that ensured my mobility including multiple weekly visits to the chiropractor's office, and really who has time for anything else. But wait, there's more. I had relationships and relationships take time and investments. On weekends when my daughter was with her father I tried to schedule in as many friend hangouts, family visits and boyfriend time as possible. When I would think about actually writing my book I would think "Ain't nobody got time for that." I kept thinking how can I add one more thing to my plate. It stressed me out.

I remember reading somewhere that we all have the same 24 hours in our day. It is what we do with those minutes and hours that matter most. I started thinking, okay Maria, beating yourself up because you didn't accomplish X, Y and Z by this age or that date isn't creating or changing anything. And who needs that extra headache of guilt or shame. Time is just a concept to God and something we use in order to compartmentalize our lives. I can start over or get started at any time, on any day, regardless of where I am right now.

So I did. I began blocking my time. With everything in me I stuck to those time blocks as much as possible in order to do the things that needed to get done. I would look at my available hours and decide what would take priority for that time and settle on 1-2 things only. That allowed me to have some flexibility if something didn't go according to plan and reduced my chances of getting frustrated. I learned that sometimes I had to shut off my phone. Sometimes I even had to leave the dishes in the sink. Gasp. Overnight. Gasp. When I did though, it freed up my time to do the really important things in life, like spend uninterrupted quality play time with my daughter, or write this book.

Another time tip that I will share when it comes to housework is what I call the Time Game. The house needs to get picked up and cleaned and other than my daughter, I had other responsibilities and passions that I wanted to take care of as well. Be it a book I wanted to read, a poem I wanted to finish or choreography I wanted to create, I needed a plan to make time for that after my chores were done.

Here is how you play the Time Game. (And notice I wrote play. Doesn't it already seem more fun than regular chores? It did for me.)

1. Assess what needs to get done around the house and what you want to do after. Make a list.
2. Start with a few short minutes of gratitude for your chores. Thank God for all of your clothes (laundry), your food (dirty dishes, pots and pans), your conveniences (dishwasher, washer, dryer), your furniture (dusting and cleaning), your home (floors), etc.
3. Decide , based on what you want to do after and how much time you have for that, on 60 or 90 minutes of chores. Or less. You decide.
4. Pick 3-4 things that need your attention that day.
5. Divide your chores into either 15 or 20 minute increments.
6. Set a timer for each chore and try to complete that task in the allotted amount of time. If you get it all done in the time frame, great , move on to the next chore and start the timer over. If you don't finish within the time frame, either use the extra time from the previous chore, and if none existed, walk away. Be done and you can play again the next day.
7. Include your spouse or children in on the fun. Make it a fun contest and the winner gets rewarded with kisses.

Doing this prevents me from getting distracted because I know that I only have 15 minutes to clean the bathroom or fold the laundry. I also find that I learn to move faster because I actually enjoy beating the clock. Plugging in to my cleaning playlist also helps give me a boost of energy. When I am done I feel good that I have accomplished something in my home and honored my blessings. I then have the time that I want and need to do the things I need to do for me, for my joy and my sanity. This makes for a clean home and a happy mom.

******

Another fair warning: You have to be a little bit crazy in order for this to work. I don't mean crazy crazy. I mean a little nutty in order to go against the grain. It takes you being a little coo-coo in order for you to go against the common humdrum attitude that many people choose to suffer from. You have to be a little weird in order to see the rainbows, unicorns and glitter that is everywhere in your life. You have to be willing to see beyond your physical eyes and use your greater spiritual eyes in order to keep returning your focus to all of the wonder that life has to offer. People still look at me like I'm nuts when I say certain things or act silly and that's okay. I am a little nutty and I'm okay with me and I am happy. When I re-read these stories that I wrote to share with you, I could see the silver lining in every story. I could see the magic and the miracles that were taking place and working themselves out. Sometimes we can't see it in the moment but if our sight is set right, we will know that good is coming and it will be revealed even if it's many years after it happened.

The other thing you will need is consistency and discipline. You are going to read that over and over in this book. It is a major theme of my life. I love this one quote by Denzel Washington when he said "Goals on the road to achievement cannot be achieved without discipline and consistency. Between goals and achievement are discipline and consistency." When we decide to achieve something, no matter the time, energy or cost, and we apply discipline and consistency, others are going to tell us that we are crazy, coo-coo, and weird.

Remember, what other people think about you is none of your business! You have to be a little nutty to ignore them and push past their words in order to make your greatness your everyday way of living and in order to live in super sparkly everything.

Make It Real.

To do the work required in this book you will need pen and paper, preferably a notebook or journal where you can keep everything in one place. Other than that what you need is time, the decision to act starting today, faith that all of your hard work will pay off, and consistency and discipline.

Here's what I discovered about time. We have all been awarded the same number of hours in a day and some use it productively and others squander it by getting caught up in time suckers. Someone brilliant once stated that we make time for the things that are important to us. That is such a true statement. You may not want to hear this but things like television, the internet and social media are prime examples of today's leading time suckers. This is the part where you need to pull out that journal and pen that we talked about earlier and figure out what you actually do with your time.

Can we be real for a minute? Do you not have time to exercise, something that will benefit your body and has incredible effects on your mentality, but you watch an hour of television every night? Do you want to finish that book you started or read the bible every morning but wake up, reach for your phone and check in to see what everyone else is doing on social media? Do you claim to not have the time to start that project that is on your heart that you know will create positive effects in the lives of others, but spend a few hours browsing the internet, catching up on celebrity gossip or reading about the news of the world that the media intentionally portrays as depressing and dismal? Do you spend minutes, hours or sometimes days worth of thought and energy worrying about something that you can't control or change instead of using that time to build your relationship with your maker, in meditation and/or in prayer?

You can go ahead and answer those questions. This is not a test or an accusation. This is an assessment to see where you are and what your excuses are. Yes, excuses. Now please understand that there is a necessity for down time and for doing things that bring us joy, as we will discuss in a future chapter. That's not what I am talking about here. I am talking about the productive use of the hours that you have been given to create the thoughts, actions and life that you are equipped to create. I am talking about making sure that we are using the minutes to contribute to the years of our lives in a positive and productive way. I am talking about the ripple effects that our actions will have on our children and all of those around us. The only real difference between the people that get it done and the people that talk about one day getting to it, is the decision to be about the business of doing and using time wisely. That may mean that it is going to take a little longer for someone who has many demands on their life. If you have children, a spouse, someone that you take care of, a job, etc, you will obviously have less free time than someone that doesn't have all of those additional responsibilities. Yet, that doesn't mean that you have no time. Be clear about that. Toni Morrison wrote the book Beloved in 30 minute increments every morning before she woke up her children and went to work. You can't finish what you don't start so, you have to start. In small increments and in baby steps.

Glitter Everywhere

Thanks to the wonderful Tony Robbins I was challenged to look at my day and document what I do with my time. When I identified the areas where I was wasting time I made a few changes. That started by my needing to make appointments with myself, intentional blocks of time designated for one specific task. I'd set a dedicated amount of time for my to-do lists tasks. Lets use my writing as an example. I would give myself an hour. Sometimes writers block would come by for an extensive visit. Regardless, I would sit for that hour and write, even if I wrote the same line over and over again. If the writers block was really bad, I would read something that usually inspires me, a la Maya Angelou or someone like that. The point is to dedicate that time to writing and creativity. Eventually the words came and stories formed. If I was so inclined I would even do more of that and less of the other things when the muse of creativity was with me. You have to carve out the time and take advantage when you are in the zone. In order to do that though, we have to be intentional about creating the space for 'the zone'.

When we make a few small changes at a time and consistent follow through with those changes, they become our new way of being. And, guess what? We won't miss those other things anymore because we instead begin to crave creating and designing our lives. That's where the real fun and fulfillment start to happen. We must thirst for ways to constantly get better, hone our skills, develop our crafts and give more. I know that this works because I did it. I still do it. I wrote the book to explain it all to you. The rest is up to you.

Chapter 6

PUT GOD FIRST Principle 1

When we put God first, all other things drop into their proper place or drop out of our lives. ~*Ezra Taft Benson*

Not So Sparkly.

The streets surrounding Topping Avenue were bustling during the late 80s. There was plenty to do for the children in the neighborhood and the choices were vast. One could decide to begin exploring entrepreneurial skills and pharmaceuticals by selling drugs, or oneself. If that did not interest you there was always the option of hanging out at the shady park up the street, experimenting with chemistry and the human body. How else could one learn how much pot to smoke or alcohol to consume until you pass out? Seriously. If your cup of tea involved being more sober and hands on, there was always your local gangs of unlicensed kids who stole cars or invited themselves into your home to help themselves to your television, money, jewelry or sugared cereal-a luxury in poverty. There was also your usual teenage pregnancy or short stints in juvenile hall for a change of pace. My older brother was always interested in gymnastics so he and his friends found that jumping out of abandoned building windows onto maggot infested mattresses while flipping mid-air was much more cost effective and closer to home than attending class at an actual gym. It also had the added bonus of not having to submit to authority, a huge problem for many in our neighborhood.

I attended Community Elementary School #70 also known as CES-70. It was a few short, yet, dangerous blocks from our apartment building. In my mind it always seemed more like a museum than a school. There was a grand staircase and wide halls. Colorful bulletin boards decorated every bare wall, proud student art and notices spilling off of the decorated and themed boards. At the bottom of the staircase there was a wide open space, generally used for bake sales, book sales, craft sales, any sale to raise funds for the public school.

In the second grade there was an announcement made at the start of class that the new substitute teacher would be holding a dance class for any and all students interested in the bake sale area. We were asked to raise our hands if we were interested. My hand was like a rocket, shooting into the air with great force and yet effortlessly and without thought. A permission slip was passed for our parent or guardian to sign. The clock on the wall tormented me, refusing to move its hands at times, sitting very still for what seemed like forever. Finally when all of my work was done, homework assignment written out, desk cleared and backpack packed, that tortuous bell rang and I busted out of the school with such a determined walk. I forgot that I usually stopped to talk with my friends while waiting for my brother at the bottom of the grand staircase and that we walked slowly and cautiously home together because there is safety in numbers. I forgot that there was a rapist snatching girls from their walks home from school, and about the gangs of middle school girls, armed with box cutters, ready to jump you for your brand name sneakers or the label on your jeans. It slipped my mind that there was anything that existed other than my planned argument to get that permission slip signed. I'm sure that the look on my face was so intense that it may have forced someone who originally wanted to mess with me to alter their plans. This was my ticket out of that house, away from that misery, and I needed to make it happen. Nothing else mattered.

Great grades, complete chores and good behavior were promised in exchange for freedom from my home and submission to dance for 3 hours daily including Saturdays. The battle was won and I was elated. I had no idea that hard work would be so much fun. I had no idea that the quest to be the best or that such a competitive spirit lived in me. I fulfilled my share of the bargain to the 110th degree to ensure that there would never be a reason for my mother to take this away from me. This is the first time that I realized that I could innately handle high levels of stress and challenge, when I wanted something badly enough.

****

By 1988 the dance program had grown so rapidly since its inception that our team was training and rehearsing during the summer months as well. My nickname during this time was Chicken Bones because I was so skeletal. Twenty hours of intense dance and dance training weekly will keep even the most active eater slim, and hungry. The break from the house was welcomed except when I heard stories of adventures had on the block while I was breaking in my pointe shoes and bandaging bloody toes. One such story was about how one of my younger, more adventurous sisters, creatively created a swing on the fire escape of our 4 story building since the park was off limits. There was an added floor because of the superintendent's apartment which lay tucked in the basement of the building and exited in the back of the building, making it 5 stories high from the back. She scaled the sharp metal patterns that decorated the bars of the cage of the fire escape to tie a large sheet on both ends of the bar that connected that top of the cage to the building. Children from the neighborhood were boasting about how much fun they had sitting in the do-it-yourself swing, the rush from the height and the excitement of its position. I was in fact jealous and couldn't wait to get home to have my acrobatic turn. Once I got home I pleaded with my mother to let me go on the fire escape, not an unusual request from a kid in the Bronx. It was close to home, got you out of the house and out of your mother's hair. Request denied. There were chores to be done, and then dinner and bedtime.

I laid in my bed, daydreaming and listening to the snores about the house. There was a gentle tap at our room window. My best friend who lived upstairs was on the fire escape and invited me out. My mother's bed was right next to the window that led to freedom, and she woke at the slightest squeak or pin drop, a result of having five children and living in a volatile area. But, I thought it was worth a try.

Now you have to understand that our bedroom was right off of hers. I gently opened the bedroom door, which was squeaking, and she left it that way to alarm her to any of us getting up. There she was, sleeping right in front of me. I slowly tiptoed across her floor until I stood before the window. Deep breath...unlock the window gate. Deep breath...push the window gate back. Deep breath...unlock the window. Deep breath...open the window. Deep breath...prop the window open with the piece of wood because it slams shut. Deep breath...creep out window onto fire escape. Deep breath...lower window quietly. Deep breath...victory dance with Peanut on the fire escape. Deep breath...that was too easy and now I am nervous. Deep breath...ignore intuition.

We climbed up the last set of stairs to the fourth floor and visited another older friend who was often left alone by her mother. She was on the phone with a guy and Peanut and I decided to chat on the fire escape. I finally decided to try the swing. The only light in the area was that shining out from the apartment and the flickering light from the street light.

****

I remember slipping. I remember the height and the wind on my face. I remember swinging around the top of the fire escape cage. I remember the sheet, maroon with beige and tan flowers, and small green leaves on their delicate stems. I remember my hands hanging onto that sheet so tightly that it hurt. I remember seeing Peanut coming towards me, in each hand a refreshing glass of lemonade. I remember screaming, screaming with every bit of strength in me, but knowing that the sound was trapped in my own head. I remember looking up and seeing the exhausted sheet come undone and then, I remember waking up in the hospital. I remember waking in the hospital, momentarily, and being upset that they were cutting my favorite Minnie Mouse shirt off of me. I remember hearing them talk about how amazed they were that I survived such a fall. I remember thinking, right before becoming unconscious again, there must be a God.

Fast forward one week. I was released from ICU and admitted to another hospital with specialized surgeons. I clearly remember the surgeon coming in and telling me that it was too risky to operate on my spine because of my age and my frail dancer's body would not be able to handle the shock. He went on about how my nervous system was so overloaded and that's why I couldn't wear clothing, or have the sheet on my body. I could feel every touch and movement, the IV needles and the wiping of blood, as though I was being violently attacked. Placing one x-ray picture after another on the well lit board he pointed out that I had fractured my skull, broken my elbow, tore the ligaments in my left knee, and crushed seven vertebrae in my back. He stated, very plainly, that I should give up on my dreams of being a prima ballerina and pursue something different because I may never walk again, and definitely would never dance again. I cried for what felt like a month.

****

I celebrated my 11th birthday in the hospital. I spent many hours alone in that dreary hospital bed with a slab of cold steel strapped to my back, a neck brace, a contraption on my leg to stabilize my knee and various bandages and dressings. Then, there was a stern voice, "Get up." Every morning, afternoon, and night, after my meal and before my blood work, I would take my legs that were going into atrophy and throw them off the side of the bed. I would push myself up onto the handlebars of my wheelchair and will my legs to move. There was no strength to even stand so I'd fall to the floor. The nurse would come in and peel me off the floor and ask me if I want more broken bones. Each time I remember looking her in the eyes and telling her, "I'm going to walk." Her smile was always a sad one. Finally after weeks of the nurses picking me up off the floor, the doctor agreed to put me in physical therapy.

I remember learning to stand the pain so that I could stand again. I remember clutching my cracked and chipped teeth, pushing deep breaths from my nose and hearing the voice telling me to walk. I remember walking and releasing the pain. I remember the feeling of defeat when the pain would overwhelm me and I was in need of the wheelchair. I remember above all else the desire to dance.

Of course, it would take about a decade after the accident and my overcoming the impossible, to realize that there was a powerful lesson waiting to be actualized. The accident taught me that we have a choice. Although we may respect the professionals and their highly regarded education and opinions, or what they consider to be fact, we still get to choose. Sometimes social, environmental, cultural, and biological realities limit our variety of choices but they do not take away our ability to choose. I learned to be an optimist, using what I now call The Fall of '88 (the accident) as a catalyst to remind myself that all things are possible and that defeat is a choice. The Fall taught me that the capacity to overcome life's greatest challenges lies within us, and some of us just need assistance in getting there because we have been told, by words or treatment, that we can't get there or don't deserve to be there. I know that my assistance came from a higher place, a greater place. God. Sometimes we need to swing our legs off the bed and try to stand, only to fall, get picked up and do it again and again and again, until we have the strength to stand and then to walk, and then to dance. We have to start somewhere. For me, it all began with a whisper and a planted thought, and then a decision to act.

Learning Moment.

When we have our own encounter with God it becomes undeniable that God is real and God is able. He makes the impossible possible . When Jesus walked the planet He was asked what the most important commandment for living was. Without hesitation Jesus stated in Matthew 22 that the most important of all is to love God with all your heart, all your soul and all your mind. He said plainly that this is the first and the greatest commandment. What I didn't fully realize until I actually started to develop that relationship was why it was so important.

Once we find Him and take a moment to realize what He has done for us and how much He loves us, our job is to develop a relationship with Him. We do that by spending time in prayer and meditation, and in reading the bible (also referred to as the word of God, or the word). You may not have fallen off of a five story building but I am sure that something happened that you weren't sure you would get through and yet here you are, reading and surviving. Maybe you had an experience when you saw a miracle take place in someone else's life. Regardless of how you got there, you were there and you need to acknowledge that there is a power greater than you that exists and by which miracles happen and prayers are answered.

For me the answered prayer was the free dance classes that rescued me from having to spend all of my after school hours at home or even in my neighborhood. When I think about some of my peers who didn't have that and where they ended up because they got caught up in the lifestyle of the streets, I realize that dance was in fact God's way of answering even my childhood prayers. As a child who was only partly Catholic and very confused, all I knew was that if God was real why didn't He save us and why was He letting all of this bad stuff happen to us? It wasn't until I became an adult and began to understand some of the laws of the spiritual realm that I realized that we have free will. I also learned that only good and perfect things come from above and that the devil comes to steal, kill and destroy. God never said that there wouldn't be weapons formed against us, He said that they would not prosper .

If you're alive please know that bad things are going to happen in your life. That is real because we are all people, imperfect and trying to figure it out as we go along. That could be for the better or the worse. People are not perfectly consistent. I am not and if you're being honest with yourself, neither are you. We sometimes make decisions based on emotions, sometimes selfish ambition, out of anger or when we are afraid. These decisions have rippling effects. Some of our decisions affect a tremendous number of people and some affect a few people tremendously.

The one thing that I know is that there is a God who is consistent. Everything He does is based on love. Not love, the feeling, like butterflies in your stomach. But, love, the verb. Love in action. Love in truth. He loves me and wants only good for me. So, I choose to put that relationship first because it is consistent and ever-present. God is always there (wherever you're going). He is always here (in this exact moment). He is there when you lose someone you love or your unborn baby. He is there when you celebrate a moment or a life. He is there when you are trapped in your head and crying yourself to sleep. He is there when you are doing your little solo victory dance. He is always there and always here. We just don't always take the time to recognize His presence.

His presence is love. When we allow ourselves to spend time in the place of love every day, and to start the day that way, we become more able to love in action and in truth. When we become more able to love, we make better decisions and those decisions have ripple effects as well. Decisions made from love affect a tremendous number of people and affect a few people tremendously. I choose God because I choose love.

When we spend time with Him, get used to Him being around and allow ourselves the space and the patience to hear Him, we come to find that He has been and always will be there.

The most outstanding miracle of my life was when I lived after falling from a five story building. It was in that time that I acknowledged that God was in fact real and present. I decided then that I am meant to live. It wouldn't be until much later that I would discern the difference between living and being alive. Either way, prayers were answered and miracles happened because I was loved by a God, so much greater than me with a love superior to any other.

When we put our relationship with God first, in all we do, we are establishing the proper order for living. We love because HE loved us first. From that relationship, and the lessons we learn on what it really means to love, we are better at loving ourselves and at loving others, related or not. As with all relationships we are shown who we are and what areas we could improve in order to be better citizens of the world and warriors of love, the ultimate commandment of the King of all Kings.

In developing this relationship we are also opening ourselves up to be constantly reminded of who we are, whose we are, and how we are meant to live. God reminds us through prayer and through the bible that we are His children and thereby rightful proclaimers of all of the promises that make life better. In order to hear Him through prayer we must be close to Him. The bible describes His voice as the still small voice. He is whispering to you, but if you are always in the midst of chaos, be it internal or external, it is never quiet enough to hear Him. When my daughter whispers in my ear she has to stand really close to me and she cups her mouth and my ear with her hands, so as to block out other sound while she is sharing. I imagine God's voice like that. I hear Him most when I keep Him close. He can only be close when I take the time to build that relationship.

This is the only relationship that we will always have safe harbor and a place to lay our burdens down. When we spend time with someone and learn to trust them we also believe that they are going to be there for us when we need them. Well, God is always there, always safe and will always take care of us. In this place we can be raw and honest without condemnation. We can be ourselves, truly, for better or for worse, remembering that there is nothing we can do to earn his love and nothing we can do to lose it. He gives love to us freely and it can never be depleted.

Some of the promises that He is trying to share with us are peace, joy, grit, goodness, kindness, faith, health, self-control, prosperity and love. Peace is the tranquility that comes from your spirit regardless of what is happening outside of you. Joy is happiness that resides in your heart. Joy does not mean that your face is smiling 24 hours a day and 7 days a week but it does mean that you carry within yourself the ability to always return to a place of happiness and gratitude. Grit is the drive that lives in you and gives you the strength and perseverance to get through life's challenges and obstacles, as we know that they will come. It's the will, courage and determination to push through and to overcome. It is that inner drive to get up again and again. Goodness becomes a part of your character, doing what is right simply because it is right. From goodness comes kindness and the capacity to act from love towards yourself and others. Faith is believing in what can't be seen right up to the moment that it can be seen. Faith is developed overtime because it requires practice. Like muscles, the more that you exercise faith, the stronger it's gets. Eventually you get to a place where you trust God with all of your heart because faith keeps you believing for things that your eyes cannot yet see.

Health is meant to be in experienced in all areas. This includes mental, emotional, physical and spiritual health. Our relationship with God and learning about what He desires for us will help us keep our thoughts under control, providing mental and emotional stability. Physical health, movement and eating right, have great impacts on all areas of our lives. Spiritual health will strengthen as the relationship strengthens. We take daily vitamins to contribute to our physical health. It is equally important that we take a daily dose of God's word and a daily dose of prayer and meditation to develop, maintain and increase spiritual health. All things stem from spiritual health. When you are healthy spiritually it is reflected in all that you do.

Prosperity is the state of being prosperous. It is defined as success, the good life, ease, plenty, comfort, security and well-being. I get so excited thinking about my life and all of it's prosperity. Think about these simple words and their powerful implications. You are deserving of living the good life. You are deserving of a life of ease and plenty, a life of comfort and security, a life of overall well-being. That is the life that God wants us to have. So long as we put Him first, honestly and truly, keeping our minds and our actions in line with His will, His desire for us to love and be loved, we can have all of this and more. And more.

Let's talk about money for a moment here. Prosperity includes money but it is not just about the money. It is about the comfort of knowing that the money will always come as long as I put God first with my money as well. The bible says this about giving and receiving. When I began to exercise the law of giving in my life, my finances multiplied and I have been able to do things for my family and others that I would have never thought possible. I recognize that it is in the release and the trust in God that there will be a great return. Money is energy and when we circulate that energy from a place of gratitude and love, it has no option but to return to us.

We spend more waking hours preparing for, being at and coming home from our jobs. Then after the government takes their cut, we are left with what we usually look at as this sad number that quantifies our hard work. Money, for most, literally comes from their blood, sweat and tears. And now, you are reading this, questioning if I have lost my mind because I am asking you to give some of that away. Not just some, but the first. The bible says that you should seek your heart and give what is right according to you and your heavenly father. The bible says that the love of money is the root to all evil. It does not say that money is evil. We need money to eat, to keep a roof over our heads and to pay our bills. Please note that the money that we make, the job that we have, the car we drive, the roof over our heads, the clothes on our backs, all of that is a blessing bestowed by God. It is our faith that allows us to release some of what He has given us in order that He may, in accordance with the law, see that it does not have a hold on us and so that we can be open to receive even greater blessings. Even the most successful business people of the world, whether they are Christians or not, follow the law of giving and receiving. It is also known as seedtime and harvest. You will reap what you sow. To simplify, the opening that happens in your heart and in your wallet when you are able to release is the same opening by which the blessing is able to enter.

Self-control is another promise that comes from recognizing that God is in control. I am my most under control when I do what I can and surrender the rest to God. This also contributes to mental and emotional stability because when I am no longer stressing or worrying about things that are outside of my control I feel better. I have to then operate in faith, remembering that He will always take care of me. As long as I am doing my part, He can always be trusted to do His.

Love. That is a sentence, statement and promise that stands on its own. Love is sprinkled throughout this entire book. For the purposes of this section let me just state here that God's love (and his blessings because of love) is like the ocean. It is massive and abundant and cannot be depleted. It is right there though, just waiting to be seen, by the eye and the spirit, and to be received. His love, like the ocean, is there for the taking so whether you show up with a spoon or a bucket, it is there to give you exactly what you think you deserve or exactly what you need. You only have to show up. Don't be surprised though when you look down the beach and see someone else decided to show up with a tub, wanting to bathe themselves in it. And yet another, with a truck. I remember I once heard a pastor say that God is a gentleman. He will not force himself or His blessings on you. He is ever ready to bless you with what you believe you deserve. So why just show up with a spoon? Why not instead take the time to get to know Him. Get to know how much He loves you and how desperately He wants you to let Him in so He can envelope you in love and blessings and give you so much extra that you have to share. He wants you to submerge yourself in His blessings and leave the spoon in the sand. All of this comes from a relationship with God. Relationships are connections and exchanges based on time, energy and resources. Are you giving Him your time, energy and resources?

Make It Real

What exactly does a relationship with God look like? Through a lot of trial and error I was able to figure out what works best for me. You will have to do the same. Again, I can give you ideas, tips and solutions but you

ultimately must recognize that this needs to be a priority,
and then make the time to make it happen.

Hearing the word *first* makes me really want to put Him
first. I realize that I have to do that in every area of my life.
So here are my top 7 tips for how to make God first in your
life.

1. *Get a bible.* There are so many different versions. You
can find one that is dedicated to you specifically (women,
teens, mothers, fathers, etc), one that is a study bible and has
guides, one that breaks down all of the words and
meanings, or one that takes apart the message in the stories.
The bible can be found in over 100 versions and in over
2000 languages. I personally like the nostalgic feeling of
paper in my hands. If you prefer technology (books can be
cumbersome) you can download the bible app. I have
YouVersion on my phone. This app is great because it has
bible reading plans, lets me keep track of what I've read,
collects my favorite scriptures and even has a kid's version
for my daughter.

2. *Carve out dedicated time to read your bible.* I highly
recommend that you schedule it for when you first wake up.
I literally mean SCHEDULE IT. Put it in your calendar and
make it a priority. Even if it begins with 10 minutes at the
very start of the day, you are starting your day with that
connection. Most people today go straight to their phones
or devices and check in on social media. If you have that
time then you have time for God. Doing this will do more
for you, even in those few minutes, than finding out that
your friend sorted her laundry ever will. If you're not sure
where to begin and have a paper bible, most come with an
index, either in the front or the back, and/or have a reading
plan that you can follow along. On YouVersion there are
plans to help you read the entire bible in 3 months, 6

months, 1 year or 2 years. If that sounds like too great of a commitment and daunting, there are also specific devotional plans that may speak to something specific in your life. These are tidbits, a little write up and a few scriptures that give you the nice boost you need, first thing in the morning. It is your daily vitamin for the spirit in you. We schedule our appointments and this should be the most important appointment and it should be happening daily.

3. *Carve out time for meditation and prayer.* As suggested in my previous tip, you need to SCHEDULE IT. You can either choose to do this right after you read your bible or right before. I like to have my quiet time with God, mostly to thank him for another day, for giving me breath, and for the hours that he is trusting me with. I thank him for my gifts and I request to make an impact in someone's life for the better. On the morning drive, whether to school or out on the weekend, my daughter and I pray in the car. We take turns. She surprises me every time as she prays with conviction in her gratitude and with confidence in her requests. Sometimes our prayers will be laced with confusion because we don't understand why something did or didn't happen and we need comfort and reassurance. Sometimes they are sad because of something that happened and we need to share where our hearts are. God can take whatever you dish out and wants you to know that you are safe with Him. He loves you too much to ever be mad at you for your honesty. So, be honest. Always include reasons of gratitude and love in your prayer. Your prayer can be a venting session and a place to share thanks. It can be a place to express praise and love and to cry. It can be whatever you need it to be. Just be sure to take the time to pray (talk to Him) and meditate (listen to Him). Rest assured that no matter what you say in your time with Him, all things work together for good for those who believe.

4. *Listen to sermons.* They are available online and you can listen to them while you do chores, run errands or go on long drives. Be sure that what they are saying lines up with what you know to be real.

5. *Read books that support your relationship with Him.* A lot of really amazing pastors have written books designed to help you develop a deeper understanding of who He is and who you are with Him.

6. *Connect and develop relationships with like minded people.* You can learn and share with each other and when one of you is in a tough spot, you have the others to remind you of who your Heavenly Father is and all of His promises.

7. *Pray often and regularly.* Pray for and with your children, spouse, and friends. Infusing prayer into as many relationships as possible, without being aggressive or infringing on others, will help keep you in a present place of His presence.

Eventually, once this becomes a lifestyle, you will no longer need the alarm reminder as you will just do it naturally. Just like brushing your teeth. You don't need a scheduled alarm to remind you to do that but when you were learning, you did need your parent to remind you consistently so that it could become your new way of living. The more you spend time with God, the easier it becomes. When it is easy, you actually enjoy doing it. We repeat what we enjoy and start to see the benefits of it. And when He is first and you are enveloped in love, everything feels and looks better. When that starts to happen you are understanding that you can live a life of super sparkly everything.

If you are not a Christian and have another path by which you connect to your higher power, a power that cultivates, condones and celebrates all things related to love, then please find literature or listen to talks that promote that. God wants us to be surrounded by love, to be aware of love around us, to love ourselves and to love others. If it is not promoting love, then it is not of God.

Glitter Everywhere.

When I began dedicating real time to developing my relationship with God, it started as five minutes in the morning before my daughter woke up and while in the bathroom. I began by reading scriptures on a specific subject matter. I would ask, out loud, "God, what do you need me to hear today?" The first thing that came to mind, I would trust that and go to the index of my bible and find scriptures related to that. Then I would read those few scriptures and the notes that were associated with them. One scripture would stand out to me the most, either because I liked what it had to say or because it related to what I was dealing with at the time. I would write it down on a piece of paper or a sticky and take it with me for the day. That was my way of keeping myself aware and present with God throughout my day. Eventually the amount of time I contributed to this relationship increased because I noticed that it had significant impacts on my attitude and my approach for the day. Obviously when you start your day, first thing, building yourself up and being reminded that God is always there for you, you move into your day with a little extra pep in your step and with a little extra sparkle.

Keep in mind that there are going to be times when you miss a day because you overslept, or you have so much to do you forgot. The key here is to forgive yourself and pick up where you left off. I read somewhere once, if you have a flat tire do you give up and slash the other three? No. You get that one fixed and move on. God is happy to know that you noticed and he sees you and knows your heart. There is no condemnation with God. So, move on.

I began this chapter telling you about the first encounter that I had that made God real in my life. It wasn't until over a decade later that I would 'experiment' with this relationship to see what would happen. Well, after a few months of being consistent with reading, praying and meditating my spirit found a rhythm. That rhythm came with a real sense of peace and happiness when I would allow myself to reside in that place. When I allowed life to overwhelm me and would cut out that time, it would have effects on every area of my life, namely my joy. The more time I spend with God the better off I am. I am still learning and growing in this every day. God is so wonderful that there are constant revelations happening. I recognize that my ability to bounce back from tragedy or what could be seen as traumatic or dramatic, is so much faster than ever before. It now only takes me a few hours to process really bad news and although I may experience sadness or another feeling associated with the situation, my internal peace, joy and love remain. They remain within me because I remain within God.

Due to the Fall of '88 there are some residual physical issues and there are things that I can't do anymore. Rather than spend my time and energy focused on that, which will only bring sadness, misery, self-pity and depression, I focus instead on the fact that I am still alive. I have an extraordinary daughter who was a week late, when the doctors said that my spine wouldn't be able to carry her to full term. I am here when I *shouldn't* be. I am able to move and dance, freely, because my God made the impossible possible within me. This relationship has opened my eyes to that and now I live a life that is not perfect but very, very super sparkly.

Chapter 7

LOVE YOURSELF Principle 2

Love yourself and everything else falls into line. You really have to love yourself to get anything done in this world. ~Lucille Ball

Not So Sparkly.

I don't remember how old or rather how young I was. I remember that I was in elementary school. I remember that it was already happening by the time I discovered dance in the 2nd grade. My therapist said that I know somewhere in my subconscious, but it is not necessary to retrieve that information in order to heal from it. So, perhaps it's safer to not remember.

Here is what I do know. It started when I was young. All of the incidents were from the people around us, kids and adults, who should have known better. It was a time flooded with sexual abuse and incest, disrespect and generational curses. There came a time when my mother would try to put me in dresses and I would cry because I didn't want to show my legs. One boy, my stepfather's nephew, old enough to know better, told me that I was so pretty and that pretty girls like to be touched. I remember thinking that I want to be ugly. I want to be so ugly so no one will ever touch me again. I was about 6 or 7.

One evening, my friend who lived upstairs came down while my mother was out and said we were going to watch a movie and that her older brother was coming to watch us. He made my stomach feel sick because she always looked scared when he came around. I liked when he was in jail. He told us to sit on the floor in front of the tv and put the movie on. It was people having sex. There were many men and only one woman. She was smiling. I wanted to throw up. I got up to go to the bathroom and her brother told me to sit back down. He said "See, she likes it." He was sitting behind us. I kept my head up but my eyes closed. 'She doesn't like it. She doesn't like it.' I kept saying that in my head. There were weird noises and he would laugh. He said if my mother found out I watched that movie that she would beat me. He took his sister by the hand and said they had to go upstairs. She looked so sad. I cried when they left. I was 8.

About a year later, I was laying in bed because my stomach hurt. That same stepfather's nephew came into the room. He laid next to me in the bed. He started again. I tried to keep my eyes closed and pretend that it wasn't happening to me, that it wasn't real. Then something happened and I decided to fight him. Just like that, I was overcome by a sudden urge to fight back. I pushed him off of me. I smacked his face and I scratched. He hit me. He said he was stronger than me. I didn't care, I just kept fighting. I cut his face and he was bleeding a little. He ran out the room and told my mother. She got the belt and beat me. I didn't care. I was going to keep fighting him. I was 9.

There were many other incidents throughout the years. Some were worse. There were different people, males and females. I was angry. I didn't want to do my hair. I wanted to wear pants. I didn't want to be a girl. I wanted to be ugly and unattractive. I wanted to hide, be invisible, to die.

****

During my childhood I enjoyed being around my mother most when she was in between men or when they separated for whatever reason. I actually wanted to be like her when she was in that space. You see, she had transformed the tomboy of her childhood to a beautiful woman, full of radiance and life. It was evident during these sola times that she accepted herself more as well. She allowed the real version of herself to unleash itself for short periods of time. During those times her authenticity radiated itself as light and gave way to a tender glow that pierced through her fair skin and deep brown eyes. I always believed that it was that resilience and light that attracted men to her. I also believed that she was too quick to surrender her true self in an attempt to avoid an argument, keep the peace or hold onto her man. She was taught, as I was learning, that if she said less, thought less, complained less, or wanted less, perhaps he could fill her void, stay longer than the last one and she could pretend to be happy. I remember becoming angry with her whenever her fair and glowing skin would turn pale and the depths of her eyes would turn hollow. I inadvertently began to despise what I perceived to be weak and vulnerable women- someone I told myself I would never become. I wanted to be that woman that she was when her radiance filled the room like a powerful aroma, and everyone left that room with traces of her on their clothing and lingering in their hair.

****

As I watched my aunt, who is less than a decade older than me, get ready to go on a date with the new guy in her life, I felt sorry for her. I wasn't really old enough to understand why I felt that way, just that I felt that way.

"Why does it take you so long to get ready?" I ask her. After applying what seems to be her 57th layer of red lipstick, she blows herself a kiss. She does this thing where she puts her pointer finger in her mouth, holds it in place with her teeth and presses her lips firmly to her finger. My head tilts to one side and my face must be saying "what are you doing?" because she catches my reaction in the reflection. She turns to me and shows me her finger with a circle of lipstick around it. "See. This lipstick would've ended up on my teeth. It's a makeup trick." She wipes the finger lipstick on a tissue and picks up the Vaseline. She dabs her finger in it and rubs an ever so small amount on her front teeth. Again, I make the face so she turns to me and says "This way your teeth don't stick to your lips. Another trick."
Recognizing that she totally ignored my question, I ask again.
"So, why does it take you so long to get ready?" She turns around, clearly annoyed, leans back so her hands rest on and hold her up on the dresser. Her eyes roll so far back I can literally see white. Unfazed by her attitude and driven by sheer curiosity, I do not back down. "Well...?"

"Ugh, Maria. Don't you know anything? It takes time for women to get ready. You have to be presentable before you leave the house. People care what you look like. They are watching you. You can't just leave your house in regular clothes, without makeup, and always with your hair in a ponytail. You're never going to get a man like that."

After a quick glance past her I realize that she is in fact talking about me. I am wearing a grey oversized sweatshirt. It probably used to belong to my brother. All I know is that this hand me down is comfortable. My jeans are also slightly too big and the belt that I wear to keep them up pokes me every time I sit and my stomach folds. I don't own make-up. I'm only 12, and I don't think I want to. My hair, my crazy curls, that made my mother throw up her hands and tell me she was done helping with it when I was 9, can always be found in an easy and trusted ponytail.

Wanting to get back at her for her obvious insult I respond with the developmentally appropriate response of "That's stupid."

She whips back around, indicating that I have already wasted enough of her time and begins applying yet another layer of blush. "Yeah, well, if you keep thinking like that you are never going to get a man. You will just be alone forever." She tops off the line of blue eye shadow with a line of green. Yikes! She looks like a clown now. It's such a shame too because she is actually quite beautiful without all that crap hiding her true beauty.

I decide to turn back to my book and pick up where I left off. My eyes shoot up every now and again to watch her add another layer of something. After squeezing herself into a tight and little dress she adds layers of colored beaded necklaces and arranges them so that they hang at different levels. For the finishing touch, one more 'lets-just-make-sure-we-have-enough' swipe of blush. I watch sparkly little residue flicker off the end of her blush brush as she strokes up toward her ear. They land on her shoulder. Like fairy dust. Hopefully it will protect her.

The doorbell rings just in time and she yells at the top of her lungs, "I'll get it!" She is letting her little brother, my uncle, know that he needs to stay out of the living room and mind his business. I lower my crossed legs to the floor, sweep my book into my hand and quietly make my way through the beads that alert others that you have passed either into or out of the living room. I go to my usual spot on the plastic covered orange furniture. I sit at the very end of the sofa near the wall and under a tall hanging lamp. If you sit still and quiet enough some people can walk in and out of this room and not even notice you there. I pull my legs in and pull my book up to my face, just below my eyes.

My aunt, now in her high heels, strolls into the living room. She pauses at the mirror near the door, perks up her boobs and checks her teeth for lipstick. Perhaps she forgot that she already did the tricks. As her hand reaches for the door she stops and smells her armpits. I think to myself 'All that time she took and she didn't even take a shower?' Her face says she needs deodorant but she must not want to keep him waiting. She picks up one of the sofa pillows and whips her armpits with it. I am so stunned that I want to throw up and burst out in laughter all at once. I bite my lip to keep me from making a sound. She puts the pillow back, armpit side down, fluffs it as if that will make it better and opens the door.

The guy steps back, looks her up and down, licks his lips and without so much as a pleasantry or even a hello, says "Damn girl, all my boys are going to be so jealous when I show up with you."
As if this is a compliment, she smiles with all of her Vaseline and lipstick free teeth, steps back to allow him a better and fuller view, waves away his words and says "Stop it."

She should have been waving away his overpowering cologne. Maybe he forgot to shower too and this is how he is covering it up. He asks if she's ready and she says she has to grab her jacket. She saunters back toward her room, through the beads, and all the while he watches her walk away and keeps licking his lips. She should share her Vaseline. It works for chapped lips too. When she has turned into her room, hopefully applying deodorant, he starts ringing his hands, nodding his head and whispering to himself. When she reemerges he says they should head right over to the party. Right before she shuts the door she yells to her brother that she is leaving.

I get up from my quiet corner, pick up the funky pillow and walk it to my grandmother's hamper. All the while I wish I could crawl inside that hamper and get washed. I felt gross. I felt sorry for her. I felt sorry for me. I felt sorry for all women. I wasn't really old enough to understand why I felt that way, just that I felt that way.

****

The snow that fell during that winter was so frequent and friendly that it summoned all of the children out to play. Although I had the responsibility of managing the household while my mother was off in the Dominican Republic handling matters of her heart, I too could hear the promise of fun and laughter from the white blanket that gently covered the streets. I allowed my two youngest sisters to go outside and enjoy the weather. It also helped to eliminate little feet and quick hands from the kitchen as I prepared dinner. It wasn't too long after dinner was done and the table was nearly set that the two oldest girls were carrying in the horrified third. The story that I gathered in the midst of tears, screaming and frustration was as follows; terrified of how fast they were going down the hill they decided that it would be best to stop the speeding sled by crashing it into a snowbank. The youngest, who was sitting in the front of the sled, had her extended legs plunged into the banking only to have her knee meet a sharp piece of ice. I immediately directed the older two to attend to tasks while I attended to my youngest sister. After realizing the depth of the wound I knew she needed stitches and called an old friend of the family to transport us to the hospital.

Once back from the hospital everyone was fed. I then hurried the others to their bed and set the youngest up in a place where I could keep a constant eye on her while tending to the evening's cleaning duties.

Once done with his black coffee, the old friend prepared to head home. While at the door, he turned to me and in his broken English said, "Jou know somesing Maria? Jou gonna be a good wife won day." Secretly insulted, I smiled at his 'compliment'. Is this why I was taught to cook at a very young age? Or why I was always told to hold my tongue, especially in the presence of a man? Why I was yelled at when I didn't clean up after my stepfather or other men? I swallowed my disgust and anger, thanked him for his help and wished him a safe trip home.

****

Good Puerto Rican girls, we hold our tongues, especially in the presence of men. We don't talk back or challenge, especially men. We are supposed to forget who we are so that we can give these men room to be who they are. We smile and look nice all the time. No, we smile and look sexy all the time. We practice cooking because you know a way to a man's heart is through his stomach, right? Well, it is.

Learning Moment.

God tells us that we must love our neighbor AS we love ourselves. This indicates that there is a demand on us to love ourselves first. The proper order is to love God and then love ourselves. In our society we are not generally told or taught to love ourselves. We are constantly told what the standard of beauty is, that we are not smart enough or good enough and that we need to struggle to attain perfection in order to be loved or accepted. That is a lie!

God tells us that we are masterfully made. When we love ourselves and prove that with action, time and energy, we are better all around. When we truly and unconditionally love ourselves we are no longer afraid of rejection because we know in our hearts that the only one we need approval from is God. We then start to make healthier choices for ourselves and find that we are happier.

The beginning of this chapter is filled with snippets of stories from my youth that used to remind me daily that I was not worthy of love. I was reminded by what was happening around me and to me that I was not enough. Well, I believed it and not only did I not love myself but I actually believed that I was not lovable. No one would want to love a girl who had those things happen to her, who didn't look or act a certain way. And then, even worse, in an attempt to protect myself I started to convince myself that I was okay with that. I was okay with not being lovable or loved. But we all know that we, as humans, are not designed to be alone. We are however designed to love, to give and receive love in it's purest, unconditional form. How do we do that when we hurt each other, judge each other and manipulate each other? More importantly, why do we hurt, judge and manipulate each other?

One day, my daughter was off on a weekend visit with her father, and my friends were otherwise engaged so I sat with God and asked what we should do. I looked over at my bible sitting on my end table and thought 'Yeah, I'll read until I fall asleep and take a nice little nap.' I asked my usual, *God what do you need me to hear today*? I started flipping the pages. Love came to me. Okay. Great. I love love so this should be easy peasy. I found a few scriptures in the index and proceeded to read them. Then I came upon this one verse where Jesus said we should love our neighbor as we love ourselves. I went to move on to the next scripture, but I found myself returning to that one scripture. I read it again, hoping this would be sufficient. It was not. I read it over and over and then out loud. Suddenly, something clicked. It says we should love our neighbors AS we love ourselves. I felt like my brain opened up and the next breath was refreshing. I started thinking of all of the ways that we show 'love' to others or rather, the lack of love we show to others. We hurt others AS we hurt ourselves. We judge others AS we judge ourselves. We manipulate others AS we lie to ourselves. We do to others AS we do to ourselves. This scripture also says that we will only be able to love others to the degree that we love ourselves. Woah. Before I knew it I was on my bed with both my bibles, my laptop, my phone, pen and paper and my concordance (a book that has an alphabetized list of most of the keywords in the bible and all of the scriptures where that word is contained).

Like everything else in this wonderful experience called life, this is a process and requires some real discipline and consistency. Here is what came out of that study on self love.....When we love ourselves, like really love ourselves, there are some fundamental things that change how we perceive ourselves and then how we perceive others.

First and foremost, we recognize that we are imperfect and that we will never be perfect in accordance to the worldly standard. We are however perfect in the eyes of the creator and as such no longer need to struggle to attain something that isn't meant for us. I will never be her and she will never be me and thank God. She is perfect at being herself and I am perfect at being myself.And both of these selves are ever evolving and hopefully progressing and that is perfect. That is self love. When we allow ourselves to love ourselves right now in this moment, we find freedom in the surrender of some other standard.

The correct order is to love God, love ourselves and then love others. After reading a ridiculous number of scriptures of who God says I am I felt warm. I had finally found permission to love myself. Or should I say, I had finally accepted the permission to love myself because it has always been there. I hadn't always realized. This new "love myself" meant that wherever I go, I am going to show up as myself, whoever I am that day in this wonderful progress that is my life, with all of my truth, all of my quirks and all of my love because I love myself. I realized that I get to take up space without having to infringe on others. I can say no when I want to say no and yes when I want to say yes. I don't have to explain myself and if I want to be honest and open, I can be. I decide who earns the privilege to be a part of my circle, people who are honest with me, who let me be me and who love me in action, not just word. I decide what is appropriate for me with the guidance of the father because He is the only one that I need to seek approval from.

In this super sparkly place of self love there is no judgement of others because we no longer judge ourselves. There is no condemnation because we no longer hold onto shame or guilt within ourselves. There is no need to manipulate because we stop lying to ourselves. Love does not allow us to lie to ourselves. There is no competition because in love, that ocean that cannot be depleted, there is plenty for everyone. There is no hate because it cannot exist where love resides. Love creates courage in the face of fear. We are more easily able to forgive others because we forgive ourselves. Embracing the statement "I love myself" makes it easier to make better choices- in relationships, in how we spend our time, in what we let in, in what we keep out, even in what we eat and consume. People who really love themselves make smarter and safer decisions. They also equally take risks, recognizing that they cannot be rejected from outside of themselves when they are so loved from God and loved within themselves. Love operates in truth, takes responsibility for its carrier and demonstrates gratitude in all situations.

The world is looking at you and following your example on how you should be treated. They treat you exactly how you treat you. We give them permission and room to act and treat us a certain way based on what we say and do and what we do not say or do. We teach people how to treat us. As stated previously we cannot control others, only ourselves. While working at JobCorps there was an experience I'll never forget. The teacher in the next room was an artistic sweet tree-hugging type of woman. She showed love towards her students and represented for a lot of them the mother they didn't have. One day, a raving co-worker ripped into her room and demanded that she do something for him. She stood slowly from her desk, calmly walked up to that angry man, got in his face and in her usual voice said, "Do you know why people don't talk to me like that? Huh? Because I don't let them." She stated very clearly that she would not listen to anything else until he stepped out of her room, composed himself and reentered her space with respect. She also required that he apologize to her class and to her, and then they could try the whole exchange again. She explained that she was sure he had a reason to be upset, but she was not it and would not be the target. He did exactly as she said. It was beautiful to watch. In a later discussion she clarified that a lot of stress and problems are based on lack of communication or miscommunication. This stress can be eradicated if we all plainly and calmly express what we want and how, because we have the right to do so, from a place of love. When we love ourselves, we will not settle for disrespect and can demand it in a calm and sweet way. We can ask for it because we know that we are deserving and worthy of it.

Allow me to be very clear, loving yourself means you love ALL of yourself. That includes your nuances, your energy levels, every bit of your body, all that you have and all that you've earned. Loving yourself means being grateful for all that you are and all that you are not, for your past lessons, your future blessings and more importantly for your extraordinary present. As a person who has relationships, unconditional self-love means you love better. As for me, I am a better parent and I inadvertently give my daughter permission to love herself as well. Knowing that my ability to love myself will create positive ripple effects to everyone around me is the best reason to love myself.

As discussed earlier, love is a verb. It proves itself with word, action, time and energy. Make a decision to love yourself. Think about what loving yourself unconditionally will feel like, look like, sound like, taste like and smell like. Include as many of your five senses as possible. Now, realize that you don't ever have to let this go. Next, create an action plan. Dedicate your words, actions, time and energy to loving yourself. There are entire books dedicated to learning about how to love yourself, so clearly this list is not exhaustive.

Make It Real.
Here are a few steps for how to start, increase or maintain self-love. Love yourself!

1. *Spend daily time with God.* In meditation, prayer and in reading your bible. Maintaining this most important relationship will show you how God sees you and the high regard that He holds you to. You will eventually see yourself the same way. Everyone who has ever attended or watched a wedding has probably read or heard the popular 2 Corinthians 13 passage on love. It has become so commonplace that we sometimes fail to really read the words and recognize those things for and within ourselves. If you take the time to read this as a formula on how to

treat yourself, and act towards yourself, it takes on a whole new meaning. We already covered the importance of this and you were given 3 steps to make this real in Chapter 3.

2. *Guard your gates.* First and foremost, watch how you talk to and about yourself. The bible reminds us that the power of life and death are in the tongue. Speak life into your life. Protect your eyes, ears and mouth (also referred to as your gates). Only let in things that contribute to the 'I love myself' mentality. Proverbs 4:23 reminds us that we need to guard and protect our minds, what goes in and out of it, because life flows from it. Protecting your eye gates means paying attention to and then being strict about what you watch, read or look at. If you find yourself always looking at magazines or social media sites that leave you feeling wanting, those are not healthy and should be avoided. You have to pay attention to the things that trigger you and reduce your intake of that thing. Paying attention to what you are watching and the messages that you are picking up are also important. Watch your mouth! Words are very important. Be careful how you describe circumstances and yourself. It may sound cliché but look for the silver lining and focus on that. We are the first to hear our words, and our bodies and brains responds accordingly.

A lot of people look at me with their heads sideways when I tell them that I do not watch the news. Media coverage is designed to be sensational. The word NEWS in and of itself means noteworthy information. Who decides what is noteworthy to me? Does it add any benefit to my life to find out the details of a gruesome murder? No. Am I naive that murder happens? No. I just choose not to let that stuff have a space in my mind. I take responsibility by protecting my mind from worrying about these things or taking that heaviness with me to bed.

Protect your ears by paying attention to what you are listening to. If you listen to a podcast or radio show that makes you sad or angry, own that you are allowing yourself to listen to that. Is it in any way building you up, increasing your faith, or challenging you to be a better version of yourself? If your answer is no, it is time to find a replacement. Protecting your ears also includes music. Music is powerful. The bible talks about singing praises and worshipping with song. You and I both know that if you are in a bad mood you will seek out music that contributes to that mood. We have playlists for break-ups and playlists when we are in a good mood. Spend more time listening to your good mood playlist. Be sure to check out the lyrics as well as the rhythm. So many times I hear young ladies, and women, listening to songs that degrade women, disrespect them, or glamorize violence. When I point this out, I often get the response "Oh, I'm not listening to the words because I just like the beat." Whether you want to admit it or not, you are most definitely listening to the words, either consciously or subconsciously. Those messages are becoming embedded, creating ideas and programs that you begin to operate on.

The things you hear influence the way you speak. This includes what others are saying to and around you. If you're surrounding yourself with negative complainers all the time, undoubtedly it is only a matter of time before you become one of them. Please pay attention to what you are allowing yourself to take in from others. What you take in through your ear gates also influences how you speak of yourself. Are you self deprecating? Do you make yourself the butt of your jokes? Do you apologize all the time for things that do not need an apology? All of these words that leave your mouth are first heard by you. Be aware of the words you associate with yourself. Do your affirmations daily (more on affirmations in the next chapter). Read them at least twice a day. It is imperative that the things you say to and about yourself, to others and yourself, are positive and life giving.

If you are a parent please be sure to keep all of these things in mind for your children as well. What you allow them to view, the words that you say to them, what you allow them to listen to and what you even allow them to eat, will have an effect on how they think of and speak to themselves. Help them learn to love themselves by teaching them how to guard their gates, by word and in action.

3. *Lighten up*. Life is too short and you shouldn't take yourself so seriously. Include laughter and joy into your everyday life. Look for reasons to laugh and laugh as much as possible. Some medical doctors actually write prescriptions for their patients to have X amount of belly laughs per day because laughter heals. To infuse more joy into your day, make a list of all the things that you enjoy doing. Every day, as you get better at carving out some much needed *me* time, use some or all of that time to do one of the things on the list. It can be reading, painting your nails, looking at pictures of beautiful dresses, sewing, crosswords, anything that makes you feel like you, and makes you smile. Try new things. Fun, scary, young and silly stuff. Do something you enjoy everyday. Taking scheduled time for yourself on a daily basis reminds you that you are worthy and deserving. Include fun into your everyday life. Don't get too serious about what you're doing, or about yourself. We did a deep dive into the necessity for joy and happiness in Chapter 5.

4. *Enjoy the present moment!* You are happier when you allow yourself to enjoy the moment that you are in, whatever that moment is. When you set aside time for yourself, try not to be distracted by what you have to do. One strategy that has been helpful for me to remain present is to create my to-do list on actual paper. This allows me to get it out of my head. I know that the list will be waiting for me when I return from my personal time. This helps eliminate anxious feelings pertaining to my to-do list. So, give it a try. Once your mind is clear, you're able to be grateful now. Celebrate the now. Live in the now.

5. *Practice your faith!* Trust your heavenly father and know that you are so important to Him that He will never leave or abandon you. Loving yourself means knowing that you are royalty and waking up every day expecting blessings and gifts in every area of your life. It relieves you of the stress of worrying about tomorrow and opens you to the infinite abundance that God has waiting for you.

6. *Forgive yourself.* It is one of the hardest things we have to do. We have to forgive ourselves for everything that we did, didn't do or should have done. Please remember that you are not perfect and you were never designed to be. There is no condemnation in Christ. Start fresh whenever you need to. Be patient with yourself, you are a work in progress. God loves you so love yourself. Whatever it is that you have done or whoever you used to be is dead if you so choose. I have good news for you. You don't have to be that person anymore. You get to decide. Sometimes you need professional help. Seek it. But it all begins with a decision. You have to decide that you want to change your ways. You do that by forgiving yourself. You have to release yourself of all of the mistakes you made, of all the damage you caused, or the people you hurt. You may find it therapeutic

to make a list of the things that you hold against yourself. Then you take that list and find the nearest mirror. Look at yourself in that mirror and say "I forgive you for…." and fill in the rest with an item from your list. Keep going until you complete your entire list. When you are done, burn the list. The list is between you and God and there is no condemnation in Christ when you repent and release it all to Him. Another approach is to write out a list of all the things that you're holding against yourself. Then, rewrite that list by using first person sentences rooted in forgiveness (example: Maria, I forgive you for …….). Read that list to yourself in the mirror everyday. In some cases, you may want to go to the people that you hurt and apologize. I recommend that you spend some time in prayer prior to doing this. Sometimes writing a letter will suffice. Ask for forgiveness when and if you can and if it is healthy and safe. Write a letter and mail it. Apologize and move on. God has already forgiven you and yet you are choosing to hold onto that and burden yourself with it.

7. *Celebrate gratitude.* All the time. Try it right now. Take a deep breath. Look around and think of 10 things you have to be grateful for. Now take another deep breath. Take a look inside. Think of 10 things you have to be grateful for about you. For some of you this exercise will be really hard. For others, specifically those of you who practice gratitude more regularly, you are already equipped to see all of the blessings that are around you. When you spend time in that place, you start to realize how loved you are, by people and by God. Embrace it and take it in. Love yourself.

You deserve to love yourself unconditionally. You deserve to live in that amazing and wondrous place, where you actually look in the mirror and see the beauty that God sees, both externally and internally. You deserve to live every area of your life to the fullest, as promised by God. Your family deserves it. Your children deserve it. They deserve it because it will give them permission to love themselves, and to make healthy choices for themselves. Loving yourself gives you, and them, permission to stand in faith and in joy, to forgive and to heal. And above all else, loving yourself means that every person you come in contact with, whether for moments or for years, will be forever affected by the light, hope and love of God that lives in you. That is powerful and that power comes from loving yourself unconditionally. That is super sparkly everything.

****

When we truly love ourselves, we no longer look for external approval. Can you imagine? It's possible! And it's beautiful! We no longer look to others to approve of us because we love ourselves right now in this moment and recognize that this moment will change. We acknowledge that we are perfectly us. Therefore, the only approval that we need is that of our heavenly father. And, we already know that He approves of us. We already know that if we are living our lives from a place of love and gratitude, apologizing when we mess up, forgiving when it's time to forgive, and doing what is right by Him, then we're good. It's an amazing feeling of freedom. We also do not need outside approval of our bodies. We no longer hold ourselves to a ridiculous standard that the world has created. Because we love ourselves we approve of ourselves in every way, shape and form.

The wonderful flip side of this is that rejection is no longer a horrible thing. Because we are alive, and because we are people, and because we are imperfect, we're going to reject and be rejected. The great difference now is that rejection is not seen as this negative and potentially traumatic event. We begin to recognize that if we are rejected by a person or a job it does not change who we are nor how we love ourselves. We become content in knowing that wasn't the right person or job for us. Through our relationship with God, we know that the universe and all things happening around us are lining up to only give us the best in our lives. So in that rejection there is no longer a rejection. It becomes more of a favor, like "Good, that wasn't the one." Then, because we're not burdened by the heaviness of feeling rejected, we just keep moving on and trusting that God and the universe are going to line those things up for us accordingly. When we reside in a place of Godly love and self-love we reside in a place where approval and rejection are all feedback. They neither become overly positive or overly negative. Our approval comes from the greatest source, thereby there is no rejection. If another human rejects you, that is okay, because you have the approval of the most high. And being able to understand and accept that, you are getting closer to a super sparkly everything life.

Glitter Everywhere.

Growing up in a girl's body that had been violated was very confusing. I would hide myself in baggy jeans and oversized sweaters. There came a time when I would also complain to myself that my flat chest of my early teenage years would made me look like a boy. I would look for compliments from others to tell me the things I couldn't tell myself. When they did, I'd feel disgusted that I needed their compliments at all.

The men who surrounded me, family and otherwise, over appraised the external features of women. This contributed to the confusion I experienced when I tried to make sense of the messages that I lived in, and the one that lived in me. As I grew into my teens I acquired more of a taste for my own style and way of looking. I started to appreciate the high-maintenance coils that sprung from my head. I started to enjoy my freckles and even found that I was offended when someone suggested that I try using makeup to cover them.

As time progressed so did my adoration of this feature or that feature. Then one day, sometime in my early twenties, I was visiting an aunt. I stepped from the shower and encountered a dynamic sight in a mirror that engulfed the wall. It was me, fully raw, as nature intended, nude. My initial reaction resembled the one that frequently came in dressing rooms while standing under harsh fluorescent lights. Those natural reactions were to either look away or only look at the parts that I liked until the rest was covered. My eyes, almost on their own accord, drifted from the safety of my shoulder region and they were suddenly delighted. Delighted that I could finally look at myself and finally accept all of my features and curves. I stared and marveled over the cellulite under my buttocks, the awkward shape of my hips, the pot in my lower belly, the size of my breasts, the length of my toes, the pointed tip of my nose, the width of my forehead, the thickness of my hair, my cat like eyes, and my delicately small lips. It all began to work itself into a beautiful masterpiece. I could be in a painting. Suddenly, I wanted to be painted. I wanted that moment of true and pure unconditional love for my body captured so that I could always remember. I didn't want to look away. It was another fascinating evolution in my life and I finally had a full acceptance of my physical self.

I am a woman. The way God intended me to be. And I love my body. The vessel that He created for me to live my super sparkly life in. I never knew that it could be so simple to release all of the perceptions I built up from the jokes I endured at my body's expense, and the media's ideas that told me my features were all wrong. Now I see that it is all right, so alright! I think back to that moment often when I catch my naked reflection in the mirror. Now after having had a baby and having lost some elasticity here or gained some wrinkles there, I still see her as I did then. She is amazing and beautiful. She is safe, no longer needing to hide or be invisible. She is me. I get to be her and there is only one of me out there.

****

I often hear women say about themselves or other women things like, "It's my turn to be selfish." or "I have to be selfish right now." or "She is so selfish." I looked up the definition of the word selfish and found that it means to be excessively concerned with oneself. Ladies, we keep using that word but I don't think we really understand what it means. Why do we refer to ourselves in such a negative way when what we are doing is what is required for us to be our best selves? Why do we call ourselves selfish when we decide that we need to take time to either recharge, recuperate, or even relax? Why do we make it seem like those needs for us are an exception to the rule, and the only way that we're deserving of them is if we are "selfish"? Here's the truth, sometimes we need, dare I say deserve, to take the time necessary in order to recharge, recuperate and or relax. When we do, it makes us the best versions of ourselves. We are more beneficial to everyone around us when we have taken the time for ourselves. Sometimes that means taking a nap, sometimes that means going to get our nails done, sometimes that means going for a walk by ourselves, sometimes it means going away for the weekend with the ladies. It's not selfish, it's necessary.

I often think about Jesus when I think about the necessity of taking the time to take care of myself. When He decided that He needed to go away He never called

Himself selfish, nor did He ever apologize. He just went. When He needed to rest, whether there was a storm happening or not, He rested. I cannot recall once when He apologized for spending forty days in the wilderness taking time so that He could be a better person for everyone else around Him upon His return. And again, never once did He come back to apologize, ask for forgiveness, or call Himself selfish. Knowing that His life is the example that we're to follow, we must recognize that this area is no exception. There is a huge difference between taking time for ourselves and actually being selfish. Let us clearly distinguish between the two in the way that we think and in the way that we speak. Rather than saying, "It's my time to be selfish." we should be saying "I deserve this time to recuperate." When we start to do that without apology, without explanation and without negatively speaking of ourselves, we are acting out our self love and that is super sparkly everything.

****

You already know how I feel about self-love and the power that lives in that love. Let's talk about what that means in regards to our sisters, other women. We spend too much time and too much energy comparing ourselves to each other. Let's end that right here once and for all. Take a second and brace yourself because this may be hard to read. Are you ready? Okay. You will never be her. She will never be you. There is only one of you, and if you get really good at being that woman you will be the best version of yourself ever. You will be the only version of yourself ever. In trying to be like her you lose the beauty and the gifts that are in you, and you'll sacrifice being the only version of you that exists. Instead, you will be settling for being a copy of someone else, and that is just not acceptable. The wonderful thing is that because there's only one of you, you are the only one who can be you in a perfect way. I'm not talking about the world's standard of perfection. That's not a real thing and it changes from day to day. I'm talking about you. Exactly how you are right now, despite the fact that you are simultaneously changing and progressing, is the perfect version of you. You're perfectly you and no one else can be you the way you can. So from now on, instead of looking at another woman, sister, or friend, and rolling your eyes because you're hating on something that they have, or thinking they have something they don't deserve, take a moment to look inward. When we fully love ourselves in all of our glory and perfection, we can clearly see that everyone else is also deserving and worthy. As we view other women in this way we are not threatened by all they have, rather we want them to be blessed with more. We can only do that when we are fully content with all we have, knowing we're deserving and worthy of being blessed with more.

Do you get it yet? It's not until we fully love ourselves that we can love others in the same way. It is not until we are fully aware and enamored with all that makes us who we are that we can give permission to other women to do the same. Then we stop comparing and we start complimenting. You and I are not the same and we never will be. There might be some things that are similar in our lives, and the fact that we're all humans, but there are real differences between us making each of us so beautiful. I have thin lips and I love them. I won't have full lips because that's not how I'm designed to be. I'm content with my lips because they're beautiful on my perfect face. I'm not going to waste my time or my energy wishing I had someone else's fuller lips. God designed her to have fuller lips and so I'm happy because they compliment her perfect face. Mine are mine and I love them. Do you see what I'm getting at? We have to, especially as women, especially in this day and age, spend more time and energy complimenting each other rather than trying to compare or compete. And here's the thing about the competition…we made it up! It doesn't exist. There is plenty for everyone. There is an abundance of love for everyone. There is an abundance of blessings for everyone. If she gets hers it doesn't mean you can't get yours. Maybe, just maybe it means you haven't gotten yours yet because you didn't even realize that you were deserving of it. Like I've said before, God is a gentleman. He will not kick down your door. You have to be willing to let Him in. That includes letting in all of the blessings and all of the abundance. He is sitting right on the other side of that door waiting for you to accept Him.

****

In trying to protect myself from wandering hands, predatory eyes, or toxic words, I stuffed down everything in me that I believed to be feminine as a way of protecting myself. I became dark, aggressive and just wanted to fight back all the time. I believed that if I made it difficult they wouldn't want to talk to or touch me. The goal was to make myself as plain and mean as possible. And it worked. Then I realized that that person I created, that person I became, was miserable and sad. Being that person had served its protective purpose in my youth, but her time was over and it was time for the new and improved me to emerge. She wasn't brand new, but new to me because she had been hiding and wanting to be invisible.

Once all of my roles were stripped away and I was at the mercy of myself, all by myself, I realized that my true self had been waiting to emerge. I had not recognized it before because I, like my mother, kept her locked away. I knew that this woman had been there since birth. Deep in my heart, waiting for her turn. Time and experience were needed in order for me to discover her. The discovery was a refreshing eye-opener. I was initially frightened by how unique and radiant I could be. A combination of every emotion, value, ability, and aspiration awakened within me. Embracing my true self and truly loving her, would prove to be what allowed me to take on the challenges that never cease to evolve from this life. I was best in my true form, free from the constructs that limited, trapped, or scared me. You know what that appreciation of myself and self love led to...yup, you got it, super sparkly everything.

Chapter 8

CONTROL YOUR THOUGHTS Principle 3

The biggest obstacle you ever have to overcome is your mind. If you can overcome that, you can overcome anything. ~Anonymous

Not So Sparkly.
Before I got married and before I had my daughter, I used to wake up in the morning and grunt when I would see myself in the mirror. The first thing I noticed was my crazy bed hair, followed by a list of things that I could see that were "wrong" with me. That internal conversation would then lead way to all of the things that were "wrong" with me that I could not see. I could hear all of the things that were once said to me in my childhood. The problem was that I heard them, decided to own them, began to believe them and then would become them. Ugly. Stupid. Worthless. Damaged. Soon enough these repeated thoughts would make room for depression and ridiculous comparisons. Now let me be clear, I was a Christian while this was going on. I say that because I want to be clear that

when you become a Christian a magic wand isn't waved and all of your problems go away. That is not real.

I would simmer in those thoughts and allow myself to think up many more reasons to support those negative thoughts. I allowed them to play over and over in my head and would give them lots of room and space in my mind. Our minds are extraordinary machines with programs and a ridiculous amount of information. It recalls things from our far away or recent past and creates programs that we then operate from. We could be minding our own business and washing dishes when suddenly the mind pulls up a thought about something that happened to you that makes you feel bad about yourself. Where did that come from? Why is it haunting me?

I can recall a time in my life when I first moved from my mother's house, still a young teenager, and all that existed was me in my quiet apartment with my very loud and negative thoughts. I had allowed other people's ideas and statements about me to be internalized. It was depressing and the only way to shut them off was to sleep. So, I slept a lot. I remember that there was a time when I thought that it would never change and that I couldn't control my thoughts. I remember thinking that they were controlling my life and that the only way to end the thoughts would be to end my life.

****

When I found out I was pregnant, I had already broken up with him. I knew then that we were operating on different plains of living. And still, with that deafening knowledge, once I made the decision to have the baby I also made the decision to not do it alone. I didn't want to repeat the pattern of singular parenting that was so prevalent in my family. I was determined to break the cycle, even if I had to bare the majority of the work in the relationship and *fix* it.

Fast forward three months. Here we go. Another argument about something so stupid. He declared that he was going to his mother's house and stormed out, sure to slam the door behind him. My soon-to-be-husband pulled out of the driveway and left me behind, on Christmas. After a while of crying by myself, too ashamed and too embarrassed to call my family or any friends, I decided to get dressed and try to find my way to his mother's house. I didn't want to admit to anyone that I ignored their warnings and that I shouldn't marry this man. I needed to join him for several reasons; to not be alone, to keep up the pretense, and to verify that he was actually going to his mother's house because there was a lurking suspicion that he wasn't and perhaps the fight was a way to get out of the house.

After a cold compress to reduce the puffiness of my eyes and some strategic makeup application, I decided that I was ready to step into the world, under the facade of the picture perfect family. I started to head in, what I believed, was the direction of his mother's house. I had been there a few times but never really paid attention to the turns and twists once we crossed the state line. That was obvious now. I tried calling him for directions but my calls went straight to voicemail. After over an hour past the state line and not recognizing anything around me, I finally decided that I was lost. Okay Maria, breath. I decided to try another route. Another hour passed and I only became more lost. Tears streamed down and began to pour out of me without my permission. I had to pull over because I was crying so heavily.

I called out to God, apologizing for trying to make my own way. I confessed that I was lonely. I confessed that I wanted something better. Suddenly, my tears were interrupted. A fierce and penetrating force moved within me. I had felt flutters and slight interesting motions since early on in my pregnancy, but this was different. My baby was kicking me. She was moving around and making herself known. I was not alone. Instantly I placed my hands on my stomach and saluted my child. "Hi baby."

At the sound of my voice she began somersaulting, kicking, twisting and turning. Up until that point in my life, I cannot recall a time when I was more present in the very moment of my life. There was an absurd supernatural awareness of my body, of the blood moving through my veins and into hers, of my heart beat, of her heartbeat, of our connection, and of the marvel that allowed me to partake in the miracle that is life creation. My tears warped from sadness to gratitude. The blooms of happiness and a positive perspective were watered by my changing tears. When she finally settled down and relaxed, knowing that her job was done, I was ready to go home. Her presence became my Christmas present while being present. I decided to turn around and retrace my steps. I eventually found my way home. I prepared for myself and my baby a lovely dinner and we sat together and had a great time. I decided that I would enjoy my pregnancy and every moment in it because I had so much to be grateful for. I decided to surrender my mental battles to God and to press forward from a place of gratitude. It was quite super sparkly after all.

****

Learning Moment.

Let me take you ahead to when my daughter was two years old. She was a precocious little girl born with an amazing insight to understand life in a way that is supernatural. She sometimes would say things that would make me think that she had been reading up on the principles of Jesus, Buddha or the Dalai Lama. I mean really profound for a small child who was still learning how to properly brush her teeth. Yet, brushing her teeth was not as important as what she knew to be real in her spirit.

As most two year olds, she was very talkative but not able to yet fully pronounce all of her words. Some of them were too cute that I would not correct her. I'd even get irritated when someone else would try and correct her. I would ask them to leave her alone and let her learn on her own. I decided that because she was my daughter she would of course learn to be articulate. In the thought of nature vs. nurture, nurture would win here and she would eventually be able to pronounce very clearly.

When I dropped her off at daycare I would say, "Bye baby. I love you. Have a great day!" Everyday. Day in and day out. Eventually, as expected, that became her mantra as well. Only, in her usual style, there was a twist. One day I dropped her off and when I kneeled down to smother her with hugs and kisses and say my lines, she interrupted me and said "Bye baby. I lub you. Hab a day!" I giggled because you already know that I liked the mispronounced words and found them lovely and endearing. I did however feel the need to correct her last statement. She said "Hab a day!" The word *hab* didn't bother me at all. It was that she left out the adjective. Great. Have a great day. Nice. Have a nice day. So, I was going to teach her better. I said "Baby, you have to say have a *great* day, or have a *nice* day or have a *fun* day. Do you get it?" She looked at me with a brilliant smile upon her face, put her hands on my shoulders and said "No, Mom. It's hab a day. If you wan hab a good day, hab a good day. If you wan hab a great day, hab a great day. If you wan hab a bad day, hab a bad day. You choice. You get it?"

My head literally started throbbing. This two year old was telling me, with absolute certainty, that we have a choice as to the outcome of our days. I knew that of course, but, how did she know that? And how did she make it so simple to explain? She summed it all up into three words....Hab a day. No adjective. You choice.

****

Back before I was blessed with my daughter, I was at work having my monthly supervision with my supervisor. I was depressed and playing with thoughts of suicide as a way to escape my misery. Little did he know that his words would forever change my life. He had no idea what I was dealing with. He just enjoyed sharing when he learned something new that he thought could impact someone's life for the better. He was talking about yoga and meditation and mindfulness. This was well before it was cool or trending to talk about these things. He said that we get to capture our thoughts, call them out and replace them with healthier, more truthful thoughts. Obviously I thought he was crazy but for some strange reason I decided to give it a try. Later that night when I got home while getting in the shower and avoiding the mirror, I started to have those negative thoughts. I noticed that one of the thoughts about how ugly I was lingered. I imagined myself catching it in a net and telling it I was actually beautiful. This might sound weird but it laughed at me. That made me persist so I kept telling it I was beautiful and then it disappeared, the net was empty and I felt lighter.

I thought I was crazy and yet I couldn't help but laugh and cry because it was gone. I did what he said and it actually worked. I was onto something here. Every time that thought came up, I would do it again and again. What eventually happened is that it stopped lingering and then it stopped showing up all together.

Time for some mental tae kwon do. Negative thoughts will emerge. When they do many people try to squander them or shove them down. That doesn't work. What works more than anything is using mindfulness to acknowledge them. We have to call it out and then tell it it is a lie. We then speak, literally out loud, to it, and tell it what the truth is. We have to say the new truth even if we don't really believe it yet. What will happen is that your negative thoughts will, because they hate being called out, stop showing up. Because you are replacing those thoughts with the new belief the truth will show up more often in it's place, until it's the only visitor.

****

The bible states that as a man thinketh, that he is. The bible has been telling us for 2000 years what scientists are discovering in this century and that is that our thoughts control our reality. So, when we learn to control our thoughts we learn to control the course, direction and mood of our lives. What is real is that when I decided that I had enough of that way of thinking and living, I began to do some research about thoughts and life, and I kept coming across the word AFFIRMATIONS. Both spiritual and secular experts were telling me to affirm myself every morning, afternoon and night. I do enjoy a good 30 day challenge so I was ready for the task. I decided to take some quiet time after my daughter went to bed. The dishes and the laundry could wait because although I was always glad when those tasks were done, they didn't make me feel better about myself. I sat down with pen and paper and my bible app. I started by looking up scriptures that came up from google searches like *what does God say I am* and *who am I in Christ*. To my surprise and delight, positive scriptures flooded my screen. I wrote an affirmation for each one.

Some were as basic as *I am happy* and some more complex like *I operate from a place of unwavering faith*. I got so into it that I started to write affirmations based on the things that I wanted, like *I am a world traveler*. All were in the will of God and inspired by one or more of the scriptures. When I was done I had over 200 affirmations (my people don't call me 'extra' just because). I also call them my truth statements. They are the real statements that I need to tell myself, out loud, and in my head, to counter the lies that I have been replaying my whole life. Lies like *you're never going to amount to anything* became *I can do all things through Him who strengthens me*. The lie *you're ugly* became *I am beautiful on the inside and on the outside*.

"Maria, who do you think you are?" I heard this degrading question from others as a child and as a teen, and then from myself as an adult. I have a truth paragraph for that one...

I am a child of the most high God. I am royalty. As such, I am deserving and worthy of all of the greatness that life has to offer. I am here on purpose, with a purpose. I am a world changer!

Once my affirmations were complete, the next step was to read them every morning, afternoon and night. Let's be real though, I am a single mother who works and I don't always have that kind of extra time. My idea: record myself reading each affirmation with power and gratitude on my phone. I always have my phone with me so I can take them everywhere I go. I began listening to them on the drive into work in the morning. Then, I would listen while having lunch at my desk, or on a brisk walk, and at night while doing the dishes or folding the laundry. And wouldn't you know it, by the end of those thirty days I was hooked. I was hearing myself telling myself how amazing and fabulous I was and calling abundance into my life. I felt like

I could walk on water and take on the world, all because I was taking responsibility for my thoughts, for my attitude towards myself, and essentially for my life. Discipline and consistency in affirming myself has brought me to where I am today. I am happy, fulfilled, secure, peaceful and feeling more alive than ever before.

Make It Real.

I am not an exception. You can do this as well. God's promises are for ALL of us. We have to be willing to be open to it and to take responsibility for our lives, starting with our thoughts. That will include taking the time to do the work. Here are some practical tips to create your affirmations:

1. *Write your affirmations based on scriptures and the promises of God.* If you don't know what they are, it's time to get into your bible and/or get the YouVersion app. (Affirmation examples are available in Chapter 14: Extras and References.)

2. *Write your affirmations in the first person and in the present.* Even if it is not true at this exact moment (or if you don't feel it's true), the word of God says in Romans 4:17 to call things that are not as though they were. For example, *I forgive others as God has forgiven me.* Or, *I am beautiful!*

3. *Keep your list in an unforgettable, obvious and easily accessible place.* Easy access is half the battle. As a matter of fact, save a copy in your phone so it's always with you. Have one in your journal, email yourself one, record yourself saying them, etc. The more accessible they are, the more likely you're to read them.

4. *Read, or if recorded, listen to them, at least twice a day.* If you can, read them to yourself in the mirror. Always read them from a place of gratitude, as if you already have them. You get to hear yourself tell yourself how beautiful, magnificent and capable you are everyday. That is powerful!

5. *Schedule it in your calendar, set an alarm, or get a friend to do it with you so you can hold each other accountable.* I would leave a sticky on the bathroom mirror, in my car, in my lunch box and on my bedroom lamp that simply read 'affirm yourself'. Once it became routine, I didn't need them anymore.

6. *Guard your gates.* Your gates are your eyes, ears and mouth. Make sure that what you allow yourself to see, hear and say are not undoing your affirmations. What are you watching? Listening to? Saying?

7. You've probably been fighting a mental battle for years. Whatever your age, just imagine, you have been running off of that old program and those old lies for as long as you've been alive. It's going to take some time to undo that. What will help you move the process along is daily consistency, and attaching the feelings that your affirmations are already real while you're saying them. Be patient with yourself and stick to it. This is a great place to begin and consistency and discipline are necessary to win. You deserve happiness. So, START TODAY!

Glitter Everywhere.

Now when I get out of bed in the morning, my mind and my heart are overflowing with gratitude, joy and love. Love for my life, for all that I have and especially love for myself. And in that the battle is already won. When I look in the mirror all I see is all that God says is right about me. I blow that woman that I see a kiss and tell her that I love her. I always have something fun and encouraging to say to her, like, "Hey beautiful! You just keep looking younger every time I see you. I see you girl! Go ahead wit yo bad self." No kidding. That is how I talk to myself in the mirror. I express love and joy to myself and I crack myself up. You already know. It's super sparkly everything!

This includes having an attitude of gratitude. When we live our lives and operate from a place of gratitude we increase our ability to be present and to be happy. Embracing this way of living also has great effects on how we perceive our lives and the events or situations that happen in it. Regardless of how bad things seem or appear we are able to maintain our gratitude and find good in all things. I did some research and read every book I could get my hands on; secular, scientific and spiritual, to try and understand the power of gratitude and why an attitude of gratitude is the way that God wants us to live. Turns out, gratitude is transformative for the mind, body, and spirit. Gratitude is discussed more deeply in Chapter 10.

My daughter moving within me reminded me that there are so many reasons to be happy and to stay present. I was pregnant when I was previously told that I could never have a child. That was reason to celebrate. My baby was moving within and reminding me that she was there. That was another reason to rejoice. I had a car and money for gas, and could drive myself and my unborn baby home and enjoy my Christmas. Another reason to be happy. Then, when she started to grow and could barely make complete sentences, she reminded me that we get to choose.

We get to choose. We can choose to capture the lies and replace them with our truths and affirmations. We can choose what to focus on and turn a bad moment into a good one. We get to choose everyday. We have to choose everyday. Let's choose to focus on all that is good and lovely in our lives. Let's choose to surrender what to God and operate from gratitude. Let's choose happiness every single day. Like Joel Olsteen said, "Success is not the key to happiness. Happiness is always a choice. You can't wait for circumstances to get better. You have to create your own good fortune. So look for ways to be happy everyday."

Chapter 9

PROTECT YOUR TEMPLE Principle 4

Take care of your body. It's the only place you have to live. ~Jim Rohn

Not So Sparkly.

It was a regular weekly ballet class filled with bouncing 6 year olds. I had them all positioned on the floor facing the mirror, ready to learn some new steps. Suddenly, as I turned my head slightly to the right to point out a dancer's need to turn out her toes for a proper first position, a gush of burning heat tore up the left side of my neck, sent shooting pains down my left arm, covered my brain with an intense sensation that I hadn't felt in a long time and rendered me temporarily unable to move. I stood very still and waited for the pain to leave. It surged up and down, over and under my left side and felt like it was burning my muscles and bones all the while. I began to breath deeply as I did not want to alarm my dancers. I slowly brought my eyes up to the mirror, unsure of how long I had been standing there and wanting so desperately to pretend that everything was fine. It was futile though as I noticed their little faces, covered in fear and some on the verge of tears. I looked at my own reflection to see what gave it away and could see that there was no color in my flesh. So, I stood and breathed. I asked them all to sit down and do their butterfly stretches. One student asked if she should call 911. I assured them that I was okay and that I got a little pain and that I'd be better in a few moments. They tried to act relieved but not one of them took their eyes off of me during the rest of the class.

That sensation happened again a few days later. After a few weeks of increased frequency I decided to go see a spine specialist. I had a sneaking suspicion that this was from the damage that occurred from the Fall of 88. And I was right. It turned out that the very top vertebrae of my spine was pushing into the base of my skull. My vertebrae were pinching my nerves causing these "whiplash" sensations from the slightest movement in the neck. To sum it all up, I had two options. The first was to undergo a very complicated and very dangerous spine surgery that has little known success. The second was to take control of my health, fueling my bones and muscles with what they needed to operate at their best, and bringing my body weight down to what my spine could actually handle and carry.

My first thoughts went to my love for my daughter. My second went to my love of dance. I knew what I had to do. There really didn't seem to be any other options. I began researching clean eating and exercises that could help me build more muscle, at home, without taking a lot of my time. It was time for me to get to the business of taking my health seriously. The alternative was enough to make me throw away all of the processed foods in my house at that time. The bonus was that I not only lost the weight and gained the muscle that I needed to support my spine, I also started feeling even better than before. I realized that food can also increase energy and boost mood. It also supports your immune system and reduces your chances of getting sick. It is amazing what the right foods and ample movement will do for the human body, mind and spirit.

Learning Moment.

Let's talk about energy and momentum here for a moment. A lot of people say that I have a lot of energy. I agree. I do have a lot of energy. Here's what I realized. When I was depressed I had zero energy. When I was down on myself and down on my life, my energy levels were also down. During that time I didn't work out much, I ate poorly and I gained weight. As I discussed in a previous chapter the medication just made me worse. It was in taking responsibility for my mind, my thoughts and my actions that I got myself out of the depression. That included eating better and moving. It is scientifically proven that when we change our physiology (body) we change our psychology (mind). Those two things are greatly connected and yet we forget that all the time. Once I got moving, my body increased production of serotonin and endorphins which are the happy hormones. They increased my ability to be and stay happy. The more I moved the better I felt and so the more I wanted to move and the more energy I continued to feel.

You've probably heard that statement 'a body in motion stays in motion', Sir Isaac Newton's first law of inertia. We're talking about momentum and energy. You have to pull out of yourself that little bit of energy that's left to get moving. Even if it just starts with going for a walk. Even if that walk is only ten minutes. You have to start somewhere. Eventually you'll find that you feel really good about it and because of it. If it's too cold out and you can't do more than ten minutes, you could throw in a couple of stair laps in your house. If you don't have stairs try doing a specific number of squats and/or jumping jacks in a small space. If your knees bother you, sit in a chair and stand up without using your arms ten times. Put on five songs and decide to dance through all five. The point is, there's always a way to get moving regardless of the weather or any physical limitations. This is where YouTube comes in handy because there are so many workouts for every single level, in every single genre of exercise, for every person out there. You just have to find what works for you. You have to start by doing something.

A lot of those people who talk about my energy say to me, "Where do you find/get your energy? I want some of that." I want to be clear, I don't find energy. I create it inside my body. And I do that by moving and by eating foods that fuel my body rather than just feed my body. What does that mean? That means that I eat vegetables, lean proteins and fruits with every meal. I limit the amount of white, bleached, or enriched bleached carbohydrates and sugars. Those things are counterproductive for the body. The organs literally have a hard time breaking things down that are not natural, so it's wise to reduce the amount of extra work we're making our bodies and our organs do. Eating the right food creates longevity in our organs and especially in our immune system. Then because our immune system is not bogged down with processing junk food, our muscles, our organs and our entire body functions at a higher level. When our bodies function at a higher level we have more energy. When we have more energy we enjoy being active and exercising. The more we exercise, the better we feel and the happier we are. It becomes a beautiful cycle. Eventually, eating right and exercising are no longer chores. We get excited to do these things because we know and continue to reap the benefits. When eating right and exercising become our habits, we are on our way to living a super sparkly everything life with a super sparkly body.

You have probably heard the common phrase 'you are what you eat'. Well, if we eat a lot of junk food or processed foods that are filled with sugar it doesn't make us sweeter, it makes us feel like junk. That has a tremendous effect on our attitude, energy level and overall state of well being. When we fuel our bodies with the food and drinks that they need, rather than eating the food that entices the tongue, feeling better is not the only benefit. We are also able to maintain our bodies ideal weight, giving us more energy and mobility. When we move and function we want to keep moving and functioning. This creates a lovely cycle of generating energy. When we generate energy through movement we produce vital hormones that increase happiness and promote healthy choices.

Food also affects mood. For example, pineapple is a natural anti-inflammatory. I include it in my morning green drinks because it really helps me with my back situation. When I'm not in pain, my mood is happier and I am energized. Another example is protein, which improves mood and increases energy. High fiber foods increase the body's serotonin, also known as the 'feel good' chemical. Leafy greens also help combat sadness and depression. Take the time to learn about the foods that are or should be in your refrigerator and cabinets. Do not underestimate the power of food.

****

I remember the time that I was car-less and my brother offered to let me drive his Jaguar. He warned me adamantly about the type of gasoline it needed. I lived in accordance to a strict budget and decided that a few times with the cheapest gas wouldn't hurt. So I spent $20 on the cheapest gas. I hopped in the car, turned it on and put it in drive. As soon as my foot hit the pedal the car started bucking. It was jerking me around as I tried to force it to leave the gas station. It felt like the car was having a coughing fit. So, I pulled over and called my mechanic uncle. I explained what had just happened and when I told him that I was at the gas station he immediately asked me what kind of gas I put in the car. Instantly I could hear my brother's warning playing over and over in my head, and I confessed to being cheap. He gave me a lovely little speech about premium gas for premium cars as he drove to the gas station to save me, and the Jaguar. He literally had to drain the cheap gasoline from the car. We pushed it back into the pumping station and he stood over me, watching me to ensure that I gave the car what it needed. He made a statement that made me think of how we treat our bodies when it comes to food. He said something along the lines of, "You think you're saving money by putting this crap into it but in the long run you will pay even more. Don't be cheap, give it what it needs."

I love to use this analogy. Imagine that your body is a luxury automobile. Luxury cars require premium gasoline in order to run and function properly. I know that you can get more for the dollar if you go with the cheaper stuff, but in order to get the most out of this amazing vehicle (that you have spent so much on), you have to give it the best fuel. You do *that* and you greatly increase your car's lifespan. If you are good to your car, your car will be good to you. Well, your body is not that different. You can certainly feed yourself with some cheaper processed foods but then you may be causing a coughing fit. Fueling it with the highest octane foods; vegetables, fruits, proteins and water, will keep it running smoothly and increase it's lifespan. If you are good to your body, it will be good to you. Unlike a car, which can be replaced, this body is the only one you have. There are many illnesses and diseases that could be eliminated and avoided if we would pay more attention to, and more money on, the food we need. Invest now or invest later in medical bills.

****

As you know I love to dance. I love movements and as a woman who has high energy it is a requirement that I move to help deal with some of this energy. Also, as a woman with back concerns, it is a requirement that I move, exercise, eat right and rest in order to maintain my weight so that I can maintain my mobility.

Most people know that if you eat right and exercise you can maintain your ideal weight. That is pretty much common knowledge at this point. The problem is that people have a hard time either beginning or maintaining lifestyle changes. Some of us are literally running off of old programs based on how we were raised when it comes to the food that we eat and the things that we do that make us feel comfortable.

Our bodies are 70% what we eat and 30% what we do. Yes you read that correctly. It means that our bodies literally are what we eat. If we eat healthy our bodies are healthy and they reflect that. If we eat processed junk our bodies look like processed junk. I know that might be hard for some to hear, but you didn't come to this book to get it easy. You came here because you were sick and tired of being sick and tired and ready for something new. The reality is that we have to take responsibility for our bodies and protect our temples. And we do that by being realistic about what we are putting in them and doing to them.

What I have learned is that the reason why my lifestyle change and overhaul stuck, and the reason why it sticks for others, is because we got clear about the purpose or the *why* behind the *what*. Let me explain. You have to be really clear about why you want to be a certain weight. If it's just to fit into a bathing suit during the summer that might not stick. If it's because you want to live a long life, you want to stay mobile, you want to have children, you want to see those children grow up, and you want to be healthy so you can continue doing the work God has called you to do, then your new habits will be more likely to stick. So I ask:

Why do you want to lose the weight?

Why do you want to gain weight?

Why do you want to get stronger?

Why do you want to get leaner?

What is your goal and why do you want to do it?

If you come back with the 'I want to fit into a bikini' answer, then I'm going to invite you to go deeper than that.

Why is it important that you fit into a bikini?

What will that do for you?

How will it make you feel?

Why is that important to you?

You must ask yourself these questions until you get to the real and honest answer behind the why. It is in that answer that you will discover your true and lasting motivation to make a lifestyle change.

Once you get very clear on why you want to do it and what you want to do your next step is to figure out how you're going to do it. Every exercise program that is out there in the world works. That's right. They all work so long as you work the program. The programs work with consistency and discipline. So now you have to go about the business of finding out what works for you. The only way to do that is to get up off the couch and get to work. You don't need to go to a gym to get a great workout. You also don't need to spend two hours out of your day to get a great workout. There are millions of exercise videos on YouTube and on cable television. Figure out what you like and what you don't like to do. Try new things you aren't sure about. Try everything. Once you discover what you like and what is fun for you, commit!

****

      In terms of food I started to make the necessary changes slowly because I know that change is only sustainable in small doses. If you've dealt with something traumatic, then an overhaul of multiple changes can work and stick. For example, I know a man who was diabetic and went to see his doctor. He was told that if he didn't make some significant and immediate lifestyle changes, he was on the course to lose his leg. He immediately overhauled his entire diet, and it's been over two years that he has maintained it. He's in great shape and is no longer diabetic. Healthy eating and active living have literally altered the outcome of his life, extended his days, and made his future that much better. It is imperative that we take responsibility for what we put in our mouths and what we do with our bodies in order to be able to live the super sparkly everything life. We may not have the scary-you're-going-to-lose-your-leg motivation, but why wait for that?

      When we are healthy physically, we are also healthier in every other way. For any of you who have ever experienced any kind of real significant pain, you know that when you are in pain nothing else matters. You are not a nice person. You don't care what anybody is saying or doing. All you can focus on is the pain. When we use food and exercise to improve our physical health we not only feel better but it has ripple effects for every area of our life. The well-being of our bodies, spirits and minds are interconnected. All of these things are part of super sparkly everything life.

So here's how I started with food. I began including greater portions of vegetables into every meal of my day. I know that may sound crazy but it is totally possible. I started finding recipes online for green drinks and would include those with breakfast. Now if I go a day without my green drink I don't feel the same until I get my green drink. That drink includes spinach, kale, flaxseed, chia seed, pineapple, mango and strawberries. I use water as my base and blend it all together. I put them all in reusable jars and stick them in the freezer. I pull them out at night so they can thaw and be ready for breakfast. To start my day I have a tall glass of fruit and vegetables and hard boiled farm fresh eggs. Because I can drink more fruits and vegetables than I can consume in a salad, it's the best way for me to make sure that I'm getting the necessities that I need in every meal.

For some of you there needs to be a reduction of carbohydrates and an increase of protein if you're already doing well with the vegetables. There is a plethora of knowledge when it comes to healthy eating readily available on the internet. Be aware that not every food program works for every person. I cannot do the Atkins diet. The very idea of only eating meat and not getting my green vegetables when I know that my body was designed to consume these things that God has given us sounds crazy to me. It is also not a sustainable way to live. I never recommend that anyone completely remove any food group from their diet. In terms of snacks, denying yourself will only lead to later defeat. Be sure to treat yourself but please do so in moderation. Make sure that the healthy foods greatly outweigh the not-so-healthy foods. Make sure that you are paying attention to your body's cues as well. If you find that you feel good after eating something and then an hour later you feel gross, you should probably eliminate that food from rotation. I prefer to eat clean and to have one cheat meal per week. That works for me as I enjoy the challenge of 'earning' my sugary dessert and it ensures that I am keeping my weight at a number that my spine can handle. For some people, this will not work, because one cheat day becomes seven and seven becomes 365. Be realistic about what works for you. If you have medical conditions be sure to check with your doctor and/or a nutritionist before you start any physical program or overhaul your diet. Seeking help from a nutritionist is a great way to start for someone who has a lot of questions and specific goals in mind.

Make It Real.
Here are my top 7 tips for protecting your temple.

1. *Increase the amount of water you drink.* Your body is 70% water and needs it every day and regularly. Try to reduce the amount of juices and sodas that you drink and replace them with water. Start with one drink a day and work your way up to replacing all drinks with water.

2. *Begin menu planning your meals for the week.* You can be budget friendly by creating a menu based on the vegetables and healthy foods that are on sale that week. Schedule prep time to prepare your meals and lunches for the week. Access and preparedness are key to success.

3. *Increase your intake of vegetables and lean proteins.* Leafy greens (spinach, kale, etc) and lean proteins (lean chicken, certain freshwater fish, etc) have so many wonderful benefits to the human body and immune system. Your organs are able to break these down with more ease than

processed foods and that gives your body the energy it needs and deserves.

4. *Keep a food journal.* People who keep a food journal are 70% more likely to stick to a lifestyle change. It's your way of keeping you accountable. You will begin to pay attention to your snacking and random eating that you may not have noticed before. Listen to your body. Take note of how you feel after eating certain foods. If you pay attention, your body will tell you what foods you should avoid.

5. *Get moving.* Start moving now! Don't wait! Your body needs to move every day. Take a class, join a gym, make a plan with a friend, go for a walk, take a dance class, etc.

6. *Find creative ways to incorporate daily movement.* Take the stairs, park far from the store doors, get up and walk to a co-worker's desk rather than send another email, do jumping jacks during commercials, etc. The incredible internet is filled with awesome ideas of how to incorporate movement into your days.

7. *Get an accountability partner.* Studies have shown that 85% of people need someone else to keep them motivated and accountable to start a new lifestyle regimen. Find someone you trust who has similar interests and have scheduled check in calls or meet-ups. You can also start a Facebook page and invite others to join you. There is success in numbers.

Glitter Everywhere.

Because of my fall that happened when I was ten years old, I deal with some residual back issues. Part of what I do is a series of stretches for my entire body and then specifically for my back. I do traction for the cervical and lumbar areas of my spine. I work out and maintain my weight by watching what I eat, which eventually maintains my mobility. I do this routine in addition to preparing my meals. This process takes me about two hours a night. As a single mother, that's two hours in addition to spending time with my daughter, making dinner, cleaning up after dinner, helping with homework, trying to get some housework done, tending to the pets and preparing for the next day. Initially, even with my great motivation of maintaining my mobility, I became really irritated with the amount of time that I was spending taking care of myself because there were so many other things that seemed more important. You know, things like laundry and sweeping. I quickly realized that I was allowing myself to become frustrated about something that needed to get done. It truly was a necessity. I was being silly. So why spend time complaining about it when it needs to get done?

I didn't have to find time to get it done, I needed to make time to get it done. This meant that I needed to prioritize. Now that this is my regular routine, there are times the dishes don't get done. Sometimes the laundry piles up. But every night, I sit with my daughter to have dinner, we play together, and after she goes to bed I attend to my physical needs. When I set out to establish this new routine, I had to talk myself into being okay with taking care of my body. That parent guilt trap tried to get me but it wasn't going to beat me. Eventually I allowed myself to let go of the guilt and just enjoy the process that had to take place. I started to really enjoy the process.

****

Now it's not a chore. It's something that I enjoy doing and get to do every night for myself. Usually while I'm stretching I'm listening to something motivational.

While I'm working out I'm listening to some of my favorite upbeat music or a powerful sermon. While I do my neck and back I read, pray or meditate. It turns out that I'm actually able to multitask even when taking care of myself.

When we decide to shift our priorities to things that need to get done, which include our health and wellness, we find that we are able to make the time to get it done. It becomes something that we have to schedule. Eventually it becomes such a part of our everyday life that we just do it without the scheduled reminder. It is in those daily decisions that positive impacts are created in our lives. We are actually creating the wonderful life that we deserve. Our lives are based on our daily decisions. Have you taken the time to create a list of your priorities? What's important to you? Is it your family? Is it your health? Is it your peace of mind? Is it your spiritual connection? Is it your personal growth? Whatever is your priority should take precedence in your calendar. You can say that your family is important all you want but if your time is not invested there then that is not your reality. And your family would agree. You can say that your health is important and a priority but if you have high cholesterol or are slightly overweight then that's not real for you either. You can say personal growth is a priority but if you don't take the time to invest in yourself the energy needed to read a book, take a class, complete a seminar, then that's not real. So here's what you need to do. You need to make a list of your priorities and then you need to pull out your calendar and schedule those things into your everyday. Not once a week, every day.

If you take the first letter from the following four words you will see what is spelled out. Healthy eating active living. HEAL. God has given us everything that we need in order to heal our bodies. Remember, healthy bodies increase healthy minds. Healthy minds create healthy emotions and so on and so forth. It's time to take responsibility for your body on the inside and the out, heal it using movement and healthy foods and live in that super sparkly everything.

Chapter 10

LIFE IS A JOURNEY Principle 5

We delight in the beauty of the butterfly, but rarely admit the changes it has gone through to achieve that beauty. ~Maya Angelou

Not So Sparkly.

I was on a regular visit in a medium security prison. Just as usual I brought my canteen card, comfortable clothing in layers, and an understanding that I would be there for a long time. Something felt different about the day though. When the person I was visiting entered the visiting room he had a book in his hands. I didn't know they were allowed to carry books around. It reminded me of the movies, where the book is actually a decoy for hiding weapons or money. I thought of cutouts to hide materials, weapons or money. I laughed at the idea and wondered what he was hiding in the book. When he sat down we went through our usual pleasantries to catch up. Then he announced that he wanted to tell me about something as his hand slowly moved over and rested on the book. I let my eyes follow his hands and notice that on the spine of the book were the two words 'Holy Bible'.

Those two words reminded me of the religion of my childhood. It reminded me of yearly trips to a Catholic Church, usually on Christmas or Easter, sometimes both. We used to get all dressed up, take the train ride, sit in crowded pews, listen to old men speak in (what I later found out was) Latin, and do this weird stand, sit, kneel process. The Holy Bibles that rested in front of us were made of leather yet the pages were so fragile that they'd rip easily. I know because the first time I aggressively turned a page I ripped it right from the seam.

The only other contact I've ever had with a bible was with the one that sat open, on the same page, on a small table as a vigil to God in my mother's house. And what I knew about him according to some self righteous and super religious relatives was that he was very angry at all of us, that we're all going to hell and there was nothing we could do about it. They always spoke of the rules and regulations that were required in order to be approved by God. There was guilt, condemnation and heaviness. I didn't want to have anything to do with it. I was working on being a better person and believed that was good enough. I also believed that if God was real there should not have been so much suffering in my past.

So, there he was with his bible and this look that was somewhere in between excitement and seriousness. *He's in prison and found something that is helping him. I'll humor him,* I thought. He spoke briefly about God and Jesus. I interrupted him and told him that I can appreciate that he found something that could help him. I was clear that it wasn't for me. I even followed that up by reminding him that everyone works out and finds God when they're in prison. We made a compromise. If he remained consistent with his bible reading and 'God stuff' for six months, I'd hear him out. He scribbled something on a piece of paper, placed it in the bible like a book mark, shut the bible, laid it down and we proceeded with our visit.

Time passed and our visits proceeded as usual-canteen cards, talking, dreaming, sharing, planning, laughing, crying... the usual. Then, one day, he came into the visiting area with that same book in hand. When he sat down I quickly reminded him of our compromise. He pulled that small slip of paper from his bible and showed me that it was 6 months to the date. "Okay," I said, "I'll listen". He began to talk about this *new* God that he was introduced to and that this God is a God of pure love. He explained that the previously mentioned relatives were taught wrong about who God was and what He was about. He showed me scriptures that explained that God had plans to prosper and protect us because the devil comes to steal, kill and destroy. He told me about free will. The part that confused me the most was when he talked about God's son and the sacrifice he made for all of us. It was actually overwhelming to think about.

On the drive home I decided to make another compromise. This time, with God. I spoke to Him for the first real time in a very long time. I asked Him to reveal to me something that only He knew, that only He could share with me, that made it clear that He was real.

The next day as I drove to work I was suddenly hit with images and memories that I had suppressed since my childhood. For so long there were many things that I did to avoid the lingering residue of the abuse. I never allowed myself to make the connection between what had happened to me and my difficulty with any and all human contact. Whenever I thought about the abuse it was as if I was watching a TV show, as if it was happening to someone else. And now, for the first time, these memories were actually my own. It happened to me. Before that moment, as a way of protecting myself from emotions and from anything that may be painful, I denied myself the opportunities to cry or express any vulnerability. During that drive as the feelings flooded back, the tears were uncontrollable. Years of pent up emotion and hurt poured from my eyes. It became difficult to drive. I could only see a few feet in front of me, my tears like a monsoon rain. But the real storm was the one happening inside of me. I could not stop it. I could *hear* something in me say "I'm right here. Give it to me." It was an encounter like no other. It was as real as the car I was driving.

Many people have told me that I needed to forgive my molesters. I realized that I couldn't forgive them for something that I refused to acknowledge or process. And so, I decided at that moment to continue on my journey to learning about the truth and the love of God in order to find my healing, forgive them and myself, and strive for freedom.

There was a period of time after that encounter when I would become frustrated with other people who experienced similar childhood trauma and weren't willing to acknowledge or process it. It would take me many years before I realize that they had yet to receive their encounter. It would take me experience and time to understand that they were on their own journey and it is not my job to fast forward them to where I was. I had to constantly remind myself that with the wonderful gift of free will, God allows us to choose whether we stay stagnant or move on in our processes.

****

I don't have any tattoos but like fake tattoos. When I can't find a specific design I'm looking for I occasionally use a Sharpie to create my own temporary tattoo. I'm not recommending this for anyone because I don't know what the ink on my skin is doing to me. I do know, however, that it's a fun way of create an image or word that I can look at constantly to keep me aligned my truths and my goals. There was a time when I wrote the word *journey* on the inside of my left wrist. I wrote that specific word as a way to remind myself that I am on a journey. Life in and of itself is a journey. The destination is to arrive at the deathbed having lived a complete, fulfilled, inspiring and impactful life. The destination is to arrive at the deathbed having loved God, myself, and others. The destination is to arrive there having lived out love through word, action and time. It was a nice reminder that because life is a journey it is ever-changing. It was a great way for me to focus on the concept of the journey, and to be patient with myself. To forgive myself. To recognize that I can't hold myself to someone else's standard because I am not them and have not been on their journey. I also began to realize that everyone else is on their own journey as well. This was great for me in particular because I often found myself frustrated when people weren't where I was. In remembering that they are on their own journey I also have to recognize that they are at their own place on their own path. So although at times my path might line up with someone else's, they're still on their own journey. Their journey is from their life perspective. In doing this, I have developed patience and compassion for them as well. I am able to give them permission to be wherever they are because I do that for myself first. This is what I mean when I say #journey.

****

I am a fan of PBS. Yes, a fan of the Public Broadcasting Station. They have fun and educational shows for my daughter (without the commercials that try to convince her that she needs the latest 'whatever' to be happy), and they have some really stellar documentaries. I am also a fan of butterflies. So, when PBS aired a documentary on butterflies, you know I was right there watching.

Here was the most educational part of the documentary: there was a group of scientists who decided that they were going to *help* the butterflies by making a small slice in their cocoons so the butterflies wouldn't have to struggle to get out and could emerge more quickly. The scientists were successful and the butterflies emerged rather quickly. But when the butterflies extended their wings and took off for flight, not one of them could control their wings. As a result, they all crashed and they all ended up dying because they could not get themselves food.

The scientists found out that the butterflies, in their dark cocoons, needed to endure the struggle of getting out of the cocoon. It was in the fight, in the struggle to get out of the cocoon, that they were able to develop the strength, the muscles and the density that would later allow them to truly take flight, soar and live. I like to think that to the butterflies it isn't even a problem. It is just what needs to be done and they are excited about getting out and breaking free, and are willing to do the work so that they can take flight and live out their destiny.

****

Learning Moment #1- Everyone is on a journey.

No one's journey is inherently better or worse. It just IS. It *is* my journey and it *is* your journey and it *is* their journey. Some people take greater turns or longer detours. Some people choose to pack light and can move more quickly. Some people choose to bring everything with them from the day they were born and are bogged down by the weight of it all. Some people move swiftly and others are crawling. Some people choose to focus on the sun (or the son) and some only see the dark clouds. Some stop moving forward on their path. They invest in property, build a home and allow themselves to settle in. Others are continuously moving, taking short breaks to recharge and refuel and then getting back on their path. One is neither good nor bad, it just *is*. We get to choose how we handle our path, how much distance we will cover, the amount of luggage we bring and the type of people we travel alongside. Sometimes we cross paths and because we cannot control others we may get a hug, or better, or a bump, or worse. Sometimes there are accidents or loss on the journey. It is all a part of the journey and it is meant to be beautiful and amazing, an all encompassing adventure.

****

Whether it is ours or another's, every action has a motive. Everyone wants to be loved, validated and accepted. Most behaviors come from these desires. Lack of self-love contributes to bad choices that are actually ways of crying out to get attention or to be seen. It is essential to understand people within the systems (journey) they live in. Their systems come from their experiences, their present situation and the direction in which the person is moving. I am of the belief that if we try to understand each other and the journey, we can care for each other, empathize, sympathize and grow together. People are developed over the seconds and minutes of the lives they live. They develop (change and/or become clearer) with all of their broken pieces. If and how they choose to put those pieces back together defines an aspect of their systems. Every person is on their own journey. As am I. As are you. Let us not forget where we came from and that there was a time that we also had to go through our 'go-through'. We have to treat people with compassion remembering that they may be in the midst of their struggle. When we do that we reduce taking their actions personal.

Please note though, that we teach people how to treat us. If their behavior towards us is not in love, we do have the right to call out that behavior in truth and in love. Also, when we take on another's responses or behaviors and assume that we are the reason behind it, we carry unnecessary weight. I have learned that the majority of the time it has nothing to do with us. We just happened to be in the line of fire when that person lashed out or closed up. If that person is a real friend, they will open up and share that they are dealing with something else and feeling out of character, with or without details. If they are not your friend, your speaking up will teach them that they cannot treat you that way. Unless you are the cause and they are willing to talk it through, that behavior will not be accepted.

Make It Real #1- Everyone is on a journey.

1. *Don't assume that another's actions or ways are because of you.* Just like you have your own journey and had to have certain experiences in order to get to where you are, so do other people. Remember that. Get over yourself. If you are dealing with mature people they will talk with you if something is bothering them. If they are not very mature or are hurting and only have negative criticism for you, thank them for their feedback and move on with your handy dandy affirmation list. You cannot be all things to all people. Let it go and move on.

2. *Extend grace and patience to others and yourself.* Remember that everyone is on their journey. Pray for others as well as yourself. We never know what someone else is dealing with

on their journey and should always do our best to extend kindness and love. You should also remember that you are deserving of the same grace and patience.

3. *Remember that every action has a motive.* When we pay attention to people long enough we can begin to decipher the root cause of negative behavior. Doing this, however, doesn't mean that we have to stay around them and tolerate abusive or negative behaviors. We can walk away, pray for them and love them from a distance.

4. *Do something that is greater than yourself and contributes to making the world a better place.* On our journeys we acquire gifts and talents that are meant to be used to help others on their journeys. Don't hold back. Develop and share your gifts. In doing so your journey becomes more fulfilling and fun.

5. *Celebrate along the way.* Some of us spend so much time and energy trying to get 'there' that we forget to pause and enjoy our time along the way. Smell the roses, do a victory dance, play and enjoy your life.

6. *Read your positive scriptures and your affirmations to keep yourself in a healthy emotional and mental place.* As we travel along we are bound to run into people and situations that will try to bring us down and steer us off course. Keeping the word of God and your positive self-love truths at the forefront of your mind and heart will help you create that protective force field needed when the time arises.

7. *Help others as well as yourself.* If you see or know of another person who has fallen and needs help, reach out and help them. That may mean donating some clothes, buying some groceries or providing some other resource to

help your fellow human. You want to be sure to exercise wisdom here and not allow yourself to end up in a situation that can be unhealthy or dangerous. Always be sure to stay in tune with your needs. Remember, if you are worn out and broken down then you can't help anyone, not even yourself. Be sure to take care of yourself, recharge and refuel, so that you can continue to walk your path and help others.

Learning Moment #2- There will be struggles on the journey.

I learned so much from those seemingly delicate little butterflies. What if we started changing how we see struggles and problems and recognize that they can be opportunities instead. Yes, I wrote OPPORTUNITIES. Opportunities to show what we are made of. Opportunities to act rather than talk. Opportunities to live out our faith. Opportunities to use some of our gifts, talents and passions. Opportunities to mature and develop. Opportunities to use muscles (mind, spirit and body) that we didn't know we had, and opportunities to show how amazing our God is….to name a few. We are magnificent and strong butterflies, designed to live a beautiful life where we get to soar.

Make It Real #2- There will be struggles on the journey.

I decided that instead of creating a to-do list here, I would give you affirmations and scriptures that you can repeat regularly and as needed. I use these often as a way to change the way I think about and eventually see the struggle. When struggle hits, I always acknowledge how I feel and why. I am real about the frustration of it. Then, I step away from the problem, turn to my Bible and my affirmations, and retrain my brain about what this means to me. In doing that I then see struggle as an opportunity and I end saying "Watch what my God will do with this." My frustration then becomes excitement because I know what He has done in my life thus far, and I know His promises are to prosper me and give me a long life. So, here are a few of my favorites:

1. *You are going to have problems.* We all already know that. We should stop asking, "*Why* is this happening *to* me?" and start asking, "*What* can I learn from this happening *for* me?" AFFIRMATION: The power of Jesus and the Holy Spirit live in me. This greatness that lives in me is able to overcome and bring prosperity to me and my life.

2. *Our God is greater than anything else that can happen in our lives.* We need to stay reminded, from ourselves, that He is with us everywhere we go and wants us to prosper. He wants us to succeed and that should give us courage. AFFIRMATION: I am strong, courageous, creative, resourceful and intelligent and can handle anything life throws my way. God is with me everywhere I go.

3. *All things work together for good for them who believe.* When I review my life without my biological father I realize that it worked out in my favor that he was not around. Now, when things don't go my way, or what I think is astray, I remember this and remind myself that all things work together for good when you believe that it will work out. Then, it does. AFFIRMATION: This will turn out in my favor because I am called and I believe. All things will work together to bring what is good and pleasing into my life.

4. *Recognizing that we are able to survive even the toughest times in life should start to build our resilience and show us how strong we are.* We have to be willing to ask, "What's good about

this?" AFFIRMATION: The experiences of today develop within me the strength for tomorrow. That strength will benefit every area of my life and help me inspire the lives of others.

5. *We have to take personal responsibility and action for our lives.* When we look at a situation there are always things that we can do to change or better the situation. Sitting around complaining and worrying about it does nothing to change the situation. Instead we must spend time in prayer. We have to do what we can and then we surrender the rest to God knowing that we did our part and He will do His. AFFIRMATION: I will do what I can in every situation to the best of my ability. I will depend on God because He will always help me and strengthen me.

6. *We get to choose what we focus on. It is possible with practice.* As previously discussed when we learn to focus on what is good and positive we are calling into our lives things that are good and positive. You are a child of God, royalty. Carry your head high and act as such. Soon enough life has no choice but to align itself with your beliefs and your actions. AFFIRMATION: I am a child of the most high God. He is always for me and has plans to prosper and protect me. I stay focused on that reality for my life.

7. *Know that God always hears you and is always with you.* This reality and the practice of these statements will build your confidence. When we develop confidence we start to ask for the bigger and greater things that life has to offer us. The word says that God has given us life to live in abundance. So, we dream big and make moves in that direction. Without even knowing how or the next step, we confidently move forward, making our requests and putting God's will first. AFFIRMATION: In prayer my heavenly father hears

135

me and because I put Him first, He will fulfill my needs and the desires of my heart.

Glitter Everywhere.

I have found that the more I do this, when problems, conflicts, and struggles hit, I am able to bounce back faster than ever rather than stay in that 'woe is me/pity party/I'm the victim' place. No one wants to stay there. It's a sad and lonely and dark place. Let us instead choose to live in a place where we can say, "I know who I am and whose I am. Even while in the struggle I know that I will come through it stronger and more capable."

In order for that to happen, we have to take responsibility for our lives, our mind and even our thoughts. God never said that the weapons against us would not form, He said they would not prosper (Isaiah 54:17). What this means is that if we are alive we will have problems and struggles, yet if we change the way we see them, through disciplined action, we can begin to benefit from them. The reality is that we would not be so appreciative of what is good in our lives if we didn't experience the bad.

I want to end with this great quote by Tony Robbins. "The only problem we have is that we think we're not supposed to have problems. Problems call us to a higher level, they challenge us to be and do better, they teach us what we're made of and sculpt our souls. The moment we realize that in life there will be problems and they are not happening *to* us but rather *for* us…..Game over! We begin to win!"

Chapter 11

KNOW WHO YOU'RE WITH Principle 6

My best friend is the one who brings out the best in me. ~Henry Ford

Not So Sparkly.

"Do you like this lipstick color?" she asked as she handed me the packaged tube.

"I don't wear lipstick," I replied.

"I didn't ask you all of that. I just asked if you liked the color," she said as she snatched it from my hand. I rolled my eyes.

"What about eyeliner? Do you wear eyeliner?" This time there was agitation in her voice.

"Nope," I sharply responded.

"Your loss," she said and she tossed the lipstick, eyeliner and a mascara into her open purse.

"What are you doing?" I demanded.

"Getting what I need. Obviously. How do you think I get all my stuff?" She said it as if I should've already known the answer.

I stood there, shocked, for what felt like a lifetime. When the shock of the moment passed paranoia set in. All I kept thinking about was what would happen if she got caught. What would happen to me if she got caught and I was nearby? I knew this was wrong but didn't want to say anything to her. She was older, prettier and way cooler than I was. Her confidence was on another level. She didn't even look up as she filled her bag with cosmetics. Whether she didn't care if she got caught or she knew she wouldn't get caught, it was powerful to watch. I kept staring at her in awe and then looked up and down the aisle to see if anyone was coming. It was both thrilling and scary. When she was done *shopping* she stated, in a tone slightly louder than necessary, "They don't have what I'm looking for. Let's try another store." As we left the store she even made a pleasant comment and shared a laugh with the unknowing cashier who told us to have a nice night. As we walked through the mall I couldn't help but look over my shoulder every few seconds to see if someone was following us. She casually strolled and talked about random things and what women around us were wearing. A young woman, about her age, was walking towards us with flower print jeans. My paranoia broke for a moment and I mentioned that I liked those. As the woman got closer, my friend put out her arm and put on a warm smile to stop the woman. She asked her where she bought those jeans. The woman indicated the store and my friend suggested we go there to see if they have my size.

Once we were in the suggested store I felt relieved and a little more comfortable. I decided that we were safe because we strolled the mall for a while and no one stopped us. My heart rate started to return to normal and I was slightly surprised at how quickly I adjusted. The clothes in that store were all so fashionable and cute, and well outside of my means. My friend and I separated to look at different styles. She returned with a hand full of clothes and asked me if I was going to try anything on. "No, I can't afford any of this stuff."

"I didn't ask you all that. I asked you if you wanted to try anything on. Come on. Grab some things you like and let's play dress up," she said. She made it sound like fun and I wanted to have some fun. So, I grabbed a pair of those pretty floral jeans, a fun sweater that also had flowers on it, and a t-shirt in my size. We went into the dressing room and tried on all of the clothes. It was fun until I realized that I liked all of the items and would be leaving the store without them. It felt more like a reminder of how poor we were and I tried to avoid those reminders as much as possible. I sat in the changing room staring at the floral pants hanging from the post on the wall when my friend came barging into my dressing room. "What are you doing in here?" I asked while laughing at how crazy she is. She put her finger to her lips as if to tell me to be quiet. She then took a bobby pin from her hair and held it up to show me. She worked quickly and quietly sliding her hands all over the jeans until she found the alarm. She did this little twist and pull and the alarm came right off the pants. Once again I found myself shocked at the fact that she was about to steal and in awe of her mastery. She did the same to the sweater and the shirt. She placed the collection of alarms behind me on the dressing room seat. She whispered that I needed to put the shirt on under my sweater and the jeans on under my pants. She took the additional sweater and folded it into a tiny square and shoved it into her bag. She put the bobby pin back in her hair and slipped out as quickly as she slipped in.

I sat there with what felt like a real dilemma. I wanted these nice clothes but I didn't want to steal. My heart rate picked up and I started to sweat. I was only 13 years old and didn't want to go jail over a pair of jeans. And if my mother found out, jail would be the least of my worries. I knew better but I also wanted to impress this 20 year old that I was hanging out with. I hurried and got dressed in the layers. I felt like everyone would be able to tell and everyone could see how bulky my clothes became. As soon as I stepped out of my dressing room she was waiting right outside. She closed the curtain of the room, concealing the alarms for the moment, and said "You didn't like anything you tried on? Me either. Maybe next time." She thanked the attendant as we walked out. I wanted to run all the way home, but my much cooler and much more confident friend strolled slowly, even pausing every now and again to look as clothes on the way out. Meanwhile my heart was beating so loud that it was all that I could hear. When we were finally a safe distance from the store she leaned close and said, "Take a deep breath. It's okay. Those stores make so much money, they aren't going to miss a few things. Plus, you would pay for it if you could afford it but you can't. One day when you can afford it you can go back and buy a bunch of stuff to make up for it. Now relax before you get us caught. If we get caught your mom is going to whip your ass." She laughed lightly.

Her speech was brilliant. It made me feel as if what I did was okay. I still couldn't talk because I was focused on breathing and relaxing. On our stroll from the bus station back towards my house I asked her how long she has been doing that. She said since she was younger than I was. She explained how her friend did her the favor of teaching her how to steal so she can have what she wanted. Proudly she declared that she has never been caught and that she does it all the time. The secret, she explained, was to be nice to people and act normal, then no one will suspect you.

"How am I going to explain new clothes to my mother?" I asked frantically when I realized we were closer to home. "Heres what you do," she started to explain. "As soon as you get home say hi like you normally would and do what you'd normally do. Then go to the bathroom. Take off the extra clothes and pull off the price tags. Put the price tags in the middle of the bathroom trash. If the trash is empty tear the tags in little pieces and flush them down the toilet. Flush the toilet either way. Wash your hands. Put the clothes away in the back of your drawers. Wait a few days to pull them out. When your mom asks you about them tell her that I gave them to you because they were a gift from my aunt and I didn't like them. My mom thinks all of my clothes are from friends. It's so easy."

And just like that, it was so easy. When my mother noticed the jeans and asked about them I nervously recited the short script and it worked. I wore those jeans until the flowers faded and the zipper broke. Every time my friend and I went *shopping* I got another item for my closet and a little more confidence in my ability to steal. I knew it was wrong and every time I mentioned it to her she gave me the speech that she gave me the first time.

Then one day it happened. I didn't see or hear from her for a while so I called her house. Her brother told me the story of how she and her friend got arrested for stealing and there was video to prove it. I realized in that moment that I allowed my fear of not being liked to drive my decisions. I allowed her behavior to influence me to do the same. All I kept thinking was, I could have been with her on that day when she got arrested. I hung up the phone and said out loud to myself, "I need better friends."

Learning Moment

As you have read in previous chapters it is of the utmost importance that we love ourselves. It is important for us to fully love ourselves and to understand what that means in order to have healthy relationships. It also helps us to determine what relationships are not allowed in our life. And by relationships I mean people. This includes family. For some of you this is going to be really hard to read.

I know a lot of people stay connected to and spend time with family that don't act like family. I'm talking about the members of your blood family who are critical, condescending, negative, disrespectful, rude and can be all-around nasty. They talk down your dreams and they talk down to you. Somewhere along the lines we were taught that this is what family does and so we just have to deal with it because that's our family. What I have learned from my relationship with God is that family doesn't have to be blood related. Those people are just in your bloodline. Family are the people who are supportive, positive, respectful and generally good to be around.

I come from a very big family. However, I created a small family of people who I love and who love me. I created for myself a small group of people who I invited into my circle based on their character not based on our DNA. Those people who I allow in treat me with decency and respect, as I treat them. They are my family, some blood related and most are not. I love myself so much that I get to decide who gets to come into my circle and whether or not they're worthy of my time and more importantly of my love. Just a reminder here, I'm not talking about love in the sense of the feeling so much as I'm talking about love in the sense of the verb. My love is strong and it moves. It is in word and in action. So those who are invited into my circle, their love has to be the same. What it looks like doesn't have to be the same but it has to be strong and it has to move.

That being said I get to choose, because I love myself, not to spend my time around negative people just because I'm related to them. I get to choose to surround myself with the people who love me. I am not going to be of the naïve belief that just because they're family I have to torment myself in that way. Absolutely not. I love myself too much to put myself in that situation. The same can be said for friendships. If you hang out with a group of people who are generally negative and talk trash about other people please know that as soon as you walk away they do the same thing to you. You are not an exception to the rule. People will show you who they are. Trust that. Love yourself enough to recognize that you deserve better friendships than that. We already know that like attracts like, so when you determine that you'll only allow embrace a certain standard of friends or family members, God will send such people into your life. The better you are at being that person the more likely you are to get those kind of people.

I love me independent of you loving me. That allows me to choose who I get to spend intimate time with and invest in. I get to choose where I put my time, energy and resources.

****

Look at the people you spend your time with. You need to surround yourself with people who are dreamers and doers. Not one or the other. People who just dream sit around and talk a lot about their ideas for the future. People who only do, without vision, are just busy, not productive. They are usually going about the tasks of everyday life but lack vision and direction to create a fulfilling future. You need to have people in your corner who are supportive of your bigger dreams and who will hold you accountable for your actions, or lack thereof. It is a necessity that we spend the majority of our time around people who are where we want to be or at the very least, headed in the same direction.

This means that we not only have to check who we are around but we have to start being okay with stepping away from some of them. We have to realize that they aren't all going to understand or believe in us. That's okay. They don't have to. The dream and the gifts were given to you.

You need to be okay with creating distance so that you can go further. If they're complacent and content with the humdrum life, and complaining about it, they will not be okay with you leaving that. You will hear things like "Oh, do you think your better than me or us?", "Who do you think you are?" or similar things.

Remember, they are on their own journey and we have to release them from our expectations. Then, we are able to appreciate them for what they have, or what they are contributing. Release the expectations to increase the appreciation. Once we fully understand and accept that, we'll find the freedom required to forgive and/or release them. On their own journey, they decided to pitch a tent and to settle in along the way. They saw the road ahead and thought it was too much work. You know better. What many don't realize is that the journey is an amazing adventure with no end but along the way there are extraordinary places to recharge and rest. They don't realize that you are desiring a life where you are really living and they are content with just waiting to die.

I'm going to be real with you here. It may be lonely sometimes but when you start to align your actions with your gifts and dreams, the right people will come along as well. While you are traveling alone please choose to use that time (or this time, if you are currently in it), to get to know yourself better. Use this time to get closer to God, to create healthy, disciplined rituals for yourself, and to figure out what kind of people you want in your life. We have a mandate to become the type of people that we want in our lives. Remember: like attracts like. For example, if you want ambitious, go-getter types in your life then you really need to develop your ambitious go-getter attitudes and actions. Those types of people will not invest in relationships with people who are content sitting around all day. Similarly, if you want to have kind and loving friends, you need to be kind and loving. And not just to the people who are closest to you, but to all humans. In Chapter 14: Extras and References, you will find a fun exercise that you can do to help you discover what attributes you want to adopt in order to become the best version of yourself.

****

Make It Real.

While you are on your wonderful adventure-filled journey, you're going to pick up relationships. Healthy relationships are really important. I know that you're thinking *duh, Maria*. And I know it sounds so simple but I have found that a lot of people don't have them and don't know how to assess if the ones that they do have are healthy or not. We need to ensure that our closest relationships- friendships, family, partners, and lovers, are safe in every sense of the word. You also want to ensure that by participating in these relationships you are able to stay true and honest with yourself. These relationships should promote your love to your greater source, to yourself and to each other. Healthy relationships push you to be the best version of yourself for yourself and for each other. They inspire you.

Rather than spend the time and the words focusing on what is an unhealthy relationship, let us focus on what is a healthy relationship. Here are some great questions to help you discern whether your relationships, be it intimate or friendships, are healthy. Please keep in mind that healthy relationships require a partnership. It's not what one person is or isn't doing. It's about what both are doing and allowing to occur in the relationships. When asking these questions be sure to ask them of yourself first before you ask them of the other person in your relationship. Also, be sure to remember that no one is perfect and that we will occasionally need to apologize and forgive.

1. *Do you seek to understand and know each other?* Doing this requires that you take the time to share your true self and give permission for the other person to do the same. It also requires that during a miscommunication you seek to understand the other person's words, actions and motives in order to fully understand the root of the conflict. Open communication is necessary in order for that to be accomplished. There's also a certain level of suspending one's own feelings temporarily so that the proper questions can be asked. This will provide a deeper understanding of each other without instant judgement or offense.

2. *Do you treat each other with kindness, gratitude, respect and love?* Because all healthy relationships are a two-way street it is necessary that both parties treat each other with kindness. It is also necessary that both parties recognize that the other has something to bring to the table. When you do that and express appreciation for each other, it helps align positivity in the relationship. As humans we tend to respect and take great care of the things we appreciate. Other humans should be treated no differently. Respect and love are also very important in every relationship. Where kindness is present generally respect also exists because those two virtues go hand in hand. But as we all know, there is a way to be kind and fake. Coupling kindness with respect means treating each other kindly because there is a true admiration for each other's abilities and qualities. And of course, you must act from a place of love, as a verb, in action for yourself and the other person.

3. *Do you freely apologize and openly forgive each other?* The wonderful and painful thing about relationships is that

they're with other people. By nature people are imperfect. We all are. We make mistakes. We offend. We disrespect. We hurt others when we're hurting. Sometimes we do these things intentionally and sometimes it's done subconsciously. Sometimes it's not intentional or subconscious, it is just perceived that way. Either way, it happens because we are imperfect. So the question here is are we capable in our relationships of apologizing when we have made mistakes? Are we capable of forgiving when someone else has apologized to us?

Now please understand that patterns are very important. If someone is continuously hurting us, lying to us, disrespecting us, manipulating us, etc., we get to determine whether or not that behavior is welcomed in our lives. If it's a pattern of the other person we need to consider that the pattern will continue. There is a way to extend grace and mercy and to forgive while also releasing that person. If one day they get healthy enough to be back in our lives, trust that God will restore that relationship. In the meantime, we have to take responsibility and stop allowing people to abuse us. This is why maintaining self-love is so important. It does not tolerate behaviors from others that lead us to betray our self-value or our standards.

If you are in a relationship with someone who does not have unhealthy patterns but makes a mistake and legitimately apologizes (and demonstrates an effort to not repeat the mistake), you have to be willing to extend forgiveness. When you do that and choose to stay in a relationship, it's imperative that you refrain from bringing up the past mistakes. The same can be expected for yourselves. If you mess up and ask for forgiveness, and are sincerely working to not repeat that mistake, you should not have to be constantly reminded of the mistake that you made when you were told that you were forgiven of it. If you do that, or the other person in the party does that to you, this is where I strongly recommend some counseling. It has not been released and therefore is still a hindrance in the relationship. The relationship cannot progress with said hinderance.

4. *Do you trust each other?* Trust is the foundation of any healthy relationship. Without it that relationship will not be healthy or will come to an end. Where there is trust, there is safety. Full trust includes emotional, mental, physical, financial and spiritual components. Break the concept of trust down and ask yourself these specific questions: Do you trust each other emotionally? Do you trust each other mentally? Do you trust each other physically? Do you trust each other financially? Do you trust each other spiritually?

You can even take it one step further and ask yourself of the other person: Do I trust [insert name] with my emotions? Am I safe to be vulnerable? Ask yourself each of these questions to gain a clearer assessment of where you believe you are in that specific relationship.

In an intimate relationship all of these answers should be yes. That is not necessarily the case in friendships because discussing finances in friendships won't necessarily contribute to that relationship. However, in friendships you should be emotionally, mentally, physically and spiritually safe.

5. *Do you have the ability to disagree and even argue with each other?* Now please understand that when I say argue I'm talking about a healthy debate not a screaming match. Healthy relationships give both parties the freedom to have their perspective and to verbalize their views. In healthy relationships, you don't necessarily have to agree on every point but you definitely need the freedom to openly discuss every point. Sometimes these discussions will allow you to gather insight into how someone sees the world, and/or

how their lives up to that point led them to that perspective. That's very useful information to help you understand each other. Sometimes you're able to just agree to disagree. Shocking, right? It is possible to be in a relationship with someone who doesn't agree on every single thing that you do. That's balance. In marriage, or in an intimate relationship leading to marriage, there certainly are some core values and beliefs that need to be shared to ensure a healthy and successful marriage. I'd recommend some premarital or marital counseling if there is a need to align differences.

6. *In addition to finding joy spending time together, do you each take time for yourselves?* Healthy relationships require, as discussed in previous chapters, that each person independently pursues his or her passions and does things that they enjoy, including relaxing. Doing these things should not come with a side of guilt from the other party who wants to consume your time.

I would warn you to be very careful of someone, especially an adult, who has a really difficult time spending time alone. I'm not saying all of their time should be alone and isolated, but some time alone is necessary. If you are that person, I strongly recommend some counseling. Alone time is a great opportunity to do the things you want to do, explore your passions, relax, recharge and spend time in prayer and meditation with God. It is necessary. If you find this to be excessively difficult there is clearly a hindrance causing you to believe that without other people you lack worth.

Some time alone also helps you figure out who you are and what you want. Think of it like this, why would someone else want to spend time alone with you if you don't want to spend time alone with you. I'm just saying. On the flip side of that, you should get excited and find joy in spending time with each other. If you find it to be a chore and you have to build yourself up prior to getting together with that person, I recommend you really take the time to pray and ask for guidance in terms of the relationship.

I myself have had friends that were absolutely exhausting. I would have to start talking myself into the meet up at least two hours before it happened. I would talk myself up the whole drive there and then try to maintain while in their presence. One particular ex-friend was so negative, she was constantly complaining, and nothing was ever good enough. There was so much good in her life stemming from extraordinary blessings, but she was so caught up in the few burdens that she refused to see it. I spent years trying to get her to see it. And not just *it* being the blessings but *it* being her perspective. Every time I left a visit with her I felt mentally and spiritually drained. I finally realized that in my attempt to help her I was actually allowing myself to be drained. She is no longer in my life and my life is healthier because of it.

Please know that God is a wonderful father and never wants us to be alone. He is the father of replacements and reconciliation. He will replace any relationships that are unhealthy with healthy ones. The only way that he can do that is when we let go of the unhealthy ones and give him permission to do what he does. Shortly after the end of the previously mentioned friendship, he sent an amazing woman into my life who is positive and supportive and healthy. She is truly a godsend and we have been friends for years. I get excited to be around her and we always make a sad face when we run out of time to be together. Yet we get excited for the distance because we know when we get back together we will have more stories to share. We will be more filled up and have more to give to each other. That's speaking to friendships. The same should also be true for your intimate relationships, if not more so, because those relationships are either marriages or leading to marriages.

Naturally in that case you will spend more time together because of the dynamic of that relationship. Keep in mind though that for either type of relationship, it is still important that you spend healthy time apart.

7. Do you like yourself in the context of the relationship? I remember a conversation that I had with one of my siblings. She said, "I don't like myself when I'm around so and so." I didn't really understand what she meant so I asked her to explain. She stated that she realized when she spends time around this certain person she is less of herself. Again, I asked her to explain. She said that she doesn't feel as though she can be her real true self because this person was very judgmental and critical. I asked her if this person was very judgmental and critical of her and she said, "Well, in general." We talked about evaluating whether or not that was a healthy relationship to continue. As adults we get to choose who we spend our time with. That includes family. If being around them makes us feel depleted (as my previously discussed friendship) or makes you feel like less than yourself, two things need to happen. First, you need to take personal responsibility and recognize that no one can make you feel less than yourself. You have to willingly give that power away and conversely you get to willingly take it back. Second, if in that relationship you are not given the permission to be your full, true, great, fantastic self then you must also decide whether or not to continue in that relationship. If in the relationship you feel like your best self and have the freedom to be your worst self (without stepping on anyone else), that's a healthy place to be.

Glitter Everywhere.

One quick reminder about relationships: Like attracts like. You have to be the type of person you want to attract in order to attract those people into your life. If you look at the types of people you are attracting and discover that you don't like what you're attracting, look at the common denominator. That is you dear. You are the common denominator. Be better and you'll attract better. When you know better, do better. Do not allow yourself to lower your values and standards for the approval of others. Know your value and you will attract others who value you. Set some clear standards and you will attract others who appreciate and honor those standards.

It takes time to develop trust. We should be our most authentic selves with everyone but only transparent with a few who have proven through time can be trusted. Not everyone deserves to hear your whole story the first day that they meet you. Not everyone gets to know everything about you. That is a privilege that needs to be earned. Your job is to pray and allow yourself to be guided. Your job is to be the best friend that you can be and the best relationship partner that you can be even if you're single. Your job is to be your most authentic self and live in your truth. When you're operating on the higher level of existing in a place of positivity and joy, including in your relationships, that's super sparkly everything.

Chapter 12

YOU'RE THE HERO Principle 7

Life blooms when we take responsibility for our fulfillment experience. Let us once more take back control of our attention, attitude, and affection. Let's get our act together and be conscious joyful adults.
~Brendon Burchard

Not So Sparkly.

I remember a sweaty man's palm holding my frail little hand on top of a cold cafeteria style table. I remember the feeling of wanting to pull my hand away because his warm palm gave me chills, the kind that made me want to run and hide. I remember that I was too scared to move and all I wanted was for my feet to touch the floor. But, they just dangled there, young, thin and frightened. I remember when the guard called that the visit was over and I was beyond excited to leave. He kissed my hand to say good bye and I quickly threw my legs over the seat bench and stood up. As I walked away I wiped the kiss off on the hem of my dress, rubbing anxiously to remove it and secretly hoping he didn't see that. I didn't remember what he looked like.

****

My mother stood on the stoop of the porch, arms crossed and eyes piercing. I sat in the passenger's seat, door ajar, one foot touching the ground. I was following my mother's careful instructions just in case he tried to drive away with me. He spoke in broken English and I couldn't hear his words. All I knew about that moment was that I wanted it to end. The stench of cigarettes lingered in the air between his mouth and my nose and the urge to throw up in his shiny car was threatening. Finally, assuming he was done with my one word answers and uncomfortable with the awkward silences, he decided it was time to go. Elated, I jumped out, placing both feet firmly on the ground and was just about to shut the door when he told me that he had something for me. He reached into the back seat and grabbed a stuffed animal. It was a wore a red bow. I thanked him, threw the door shut and walked swiftly back towards my mother. Seeing that I was approaching, she lowered her arms, sighed, and headed back into the building. I looked back to make sure he had driven away. At the top of the stoop stairs, I leaned over the left side railing and dropped the innocent bear with his perfect red bowtie into the open dirty trash barrel that waited below. She never asked about the bear and I never spoke of it.

****

I snatched the form from my brother's hand, rolling my eyes as if that was the only way to keep them in my head and I wrote my name in clear and legible print, as requested. MARIA MILAGROS VAZQUEZ. After completing the form, I dropped it into my brother's lap and sarcastically muttered, "Can't wait, so excited." He chuckled and said, for what seemed to be the thousandth time, "You need this as much as I do". Almost a month later, he called me and gave me the date and time. We arranged travel plans and overnight accommodations.

The date arrived. Thoughts of him, who he is and what he looks like, we're sprinting in my mind. Suddenly I became overwhelmed with anger and thought this is probably a bad idea. Yet, there was a safety in knowing that my older and protective brother was there with me and for me.

After a thorough search of my pockets, hair, bra and shoes, we were allowed in. We had to walk through the visiting area where contact was allowed to the glassed back room where the more violent criminals had their visits. As we entered, other inmates stopped talking to their guests and stared at us. The room grew increasingly quiet and the awkward weirdness of this event gave me motion sickness. The correction officers noticed the disturbance and stood to their feet, eyes darting quickly back and forth from the inmates to us, inmates to us, and inmates to us. Finally we heard an exchange between two blue jump suited men and knew what was happening. "That has to be them. He's been talking about this all month. Look. He looks just like his father." The attention that we got from the inmates made us realize that his power behind the concrete and electric fences was all that it was rumored to be. We were placed behind double paned bullet proof glass and had to speak on a phone receiver that had a slimy film of bacteria on it. There was only one stool, and neither of us wanted to sit.

I've been told that I look just like my mother my whole life. When this distinguished Latin man approached and stood opposite me I could see his face as well as my own reflection. I look like him, the darker skin, the dark eyes, and the curly and coarse hair. The reality that this was him, this was the man that we so often referred to as the sperm donor, that this was my father, settled in an eerie knot in my stomach. My brother was a taller and lighter version but clearly his son as well.

Over the next 3 or 4 hours we never sat, never had to use the bathroom or eat. Nothing else but this moment and clearing up some past hurts mattered. We took turns on the phone, badgering this man with questions and making definitive statements about his absence, his behaviors and how it all affected us. Eventually, I realized that this sad lost little man refused to take any responsibility for his actions. He blamed my mother, who was ten years his junior when they met. He, a grown man of twenty-five, and she, an impressionable teenager at fifteen. He blamed his children, and his attempts to instill guilt for waiting so long to visit him in jail drew the ultimate line of closure. I held the infested phone away from my face, just far enough so he knew I wasn't talking directly to him, and also close enough that he could hear my every word. I glared over at my brother, "I'm done. He's doing 30 years for his what…? Third attempted murder? He takes no responsibility and has no regard for anyone except himself. I haven't needed this man these 26 years, I don't need him now." I placed the receiver back on its rusted hook and smiled at our matching faces. The smile was multifaceted and multitalented. It said 'I don't need you', and 'Take a good look because you're probably never going to see my face this close again'.

I grabbed the stool and moved it up against the back wall, sat down and let out a deep breath. My feet touched the ground. I no longer needed to run from him or this. I lifted my foot from the steady and secure safety of the floor and placed it on the bar of the stool. Then, I lifted the other.

My new way of thinking allowed me to recognize that this *bad* ended up being for my *good*, it was for my *best*. I recognized that this guy is my birth father. That is a fact. He is not a predictor of my future. That's also a fact. I let him go, finally. He is on his journey and there's no need for me to be on the road with him. All of the years of self-pity that I played into for being fatherless fell away. All of the anger melted away. I forgave him in that moment and thanked God for keeping that man from my life. Super sparkly everything.

Learning Moment.

For so long I gave away my power to the people who were there and hurt me, and to the people who weren't there but I believed should have been. It was easier to be the victim of my circumstances rather than own my life and what was becoming of it. It was easier to wait around for someone to rescue me than it was for me to become my own hero. It was definitely easier to point at my absent drug addicted criminal father and blame his absence for many things in my life that weren't going right.

It was after meeting my father and talking to him that I realized that his absence was in fact a blessing. The very thing that I believed was a hindrance turned out to be a great thing. God kept that man from my life and that protected me. That man was abusive towards my mother and blamed everyone else for his problems. I have to believe that not having a parent like that in my everyday life saved me from a potentially similar life.

This new revelation also forced me to realize that my mother really did the best she could with what she knew. Her parenting style came from her parents and although there was much to be desired in the way of love and affection, she could not give us what she never received. She was on her journey and then we came along. She did the best she could. Children don't come with a manual and she only knew what she was taught. I actually believe that she believed she was doing better than her parents did.

Make It Real.

In order for us to take responsibility for our lives and become our own heroes, we must forgive and release anyone who we hold any anger, resentment or grudges against. When we hold onto those things, we are actually exchanging our freedom for the weight and the burden of not forgiving. We must find freedom from the people or situations that keep us chained. When we do not forgive, we are chained to the past, dragging around something that we keep with us in our present, and carry into our future. We need to cut the chain and release ourselves of the hindrance. Not until we do that can we move into all of the super sparkly everything that God has waiting for us, that we deserve, that is our birthright. We must also accept the permission that we have been given to say yes to the things we want and need to do. Conversely, we can say no to the rest.

1. Forgive your parents. The first step in taking responsibility for your life is to forgive your parents (your mother, your father, any stepparents, adoptive parents, grandparents who acted as parents, etc.) Again, they probably did the best they could with what they knew. Even if they didn't forgive them so that you can be free of them. Release them and surrender them to God.

2. Forgive others. I needed to forgive my molesters. I reminded myself that they hurt me because they were hurt, perhaps in the same way, perhaps worse. Hurt people will hurt people. They have their own twisted motives. When I allow to myself remember that I can forgave them and felt compassion for them while praying for their healing. That's right, we are called to pray for their healing and for blessings

in their life. If you think about it, they weren't born that way. Bad things happened to them and people hurt them. Somewhere along their journey they got so lost in all that hurt. When we are lost we get frustrated and sometimes act out. Somewhere along the journey, those pains and frustrations started to dictate their actions.

Who do you have to forgive? Who are you still chained to and carrying into your present? Who has your power and control? Release them and release yourself. You can fly better when you don't have so much weight to carry. This doesn't mean that they need to be in your life. Forgiveness is a gift you give to yourself so that you can be free. If you struggle in this area, I recommend being very honest with God and asking Him to take this from you, to free you and then pray for them. There is such freedom in forgiveness and surrender. Remember that God loves them too so forgive them and release them. Let's be clear about 2 things:

1. *Forgiveness does not mean that what was done is okay.* It means that you have decided to stop carrying the grudge, the extra weight, the baggage that comes with holding onto the heaviness of the event. Although they are facts from your past, they don't have to be the path of your future. It releases you from letting it hinder you and hold you back.

2. *There are times during which you have to release people, who are continuously causing pain and suffering in your life.* If their presence and time in your life is toxic and/or unhealthy, you have permission to release them from your life. You absolutely can forgive them and then remove them from your present. Pray for them and send them love from a distance. Be kind and civil when you run into or encounter them. God loves them too. You cannot fix them and that is

not your job. Please know that you can't love anyone enough to change them into being good to you. Only God can do that work and it has to happen within them before it will be evident outside of them. Let them go and let God take over.

3. *Make time for self-care every single day.* Be sure that you are allowing yourself the time to keep yourself in a healthy place so that you can do all of the work that you are called to do and be all that you are called to be. As the only person who is truly responsible for your happiness, for your peace and for your story, you have to make self-care a priority.

4. *Say yes when you want to.* Try new things and step out of your comfort zone. This is a great way to find out what you are passionate about. It is also a great way to discover your purpose. You are not going to figure it out by staying in your head. You will figure it out in action. Start doing things you've wanted to do, take that class, learn that instrument, increase a skill. Say YES to life and to opportunities that line up with who you want to be, where you want to go and what you want to accomplish.

5. *Say no when you can't or when you don't want to.* Matthew 5:37 reminds us to let our yes be yes and our no be no. When you have gotten to a place of self-love and recognized your value, you will also begin to start valuing your time. You get to say no to the people, projects and distractions that take you away from who you want to be, where you want to go and what you want to accomplish.

6. *Release created expectations so that you can increase the appreciation.* Had I not released my mother of the created expectations that I had for her, of the mother she 'should have' been, I would not have been able to fully appreciate all

that she did do for us and all of the powerful life lessons that I learned from her. (like her ability to make a decision and follow through for the greater good of her children). All of those lessons contribute to who I am today for the better. Who in your life do you need to release expectations of? What did they bring into your life that you can appreciate?

7. *Invest in yourself!* That is time, money, and energy. You deserve it. Seek knowledge and understanding. Continue to learn and grow. Get help if you need it. Get a coach, mentor, counselor or a professional if that's what you need to excel in your life.

Glitter Everywhere.

You're the hero! Yes. You read that correctly. You have to take responsibility for every area of your life, like the hero does. Step in and take charge. You get to put on your super suit of love, your cape of gratitude and take charge of your life. You can't fly as high, or at all, if you are weighed down by the force that comes from not forgiving. The first step is to forgive and release anyone who came against you. Forgiving yourself for any mistakes that you made and remembering that you will make more is also a part of the journey. For some this can come with a prayer and for others it will have to come with some professional help. Taking responsibility for your life includes seeking that help if that is what you need.

On this journey that is your life, You are the only one who can free yourself from being chained to a person or an event that hinders you. You are the only person who can truly forgive you for any past mistakes that you have made, because God already has. When you look at your life, be sure to spend time thinking about the lessons from your 'traumatic' or 'tragic' events. You are the only one who gets to decide if there was a lesson there and what that lesson was. You are the only one who can grow and learn and become better from doing that work. You have in you everything that you need to live your best life regardless of your past. You get to decide because you are the lead in your story and you are the hero in your life. And, you were already given this authority because you are fully capable and resilient. Combining all that you have learned with all that you are, will help you become your best superhero ever. Or should I say, the best super sparkly hero ever.

Chapter 13

AND IN CONCLUSION

If you're waiting for a sign, if you're waiting for a signal, if you're waiting for permission, this is it! ~Maria Milagros

Another Hero Trait.

I don't remember all of the exact details of this particular story and I have a suspicion that I'm mixing several stories into one. Nonetheless, here is how I remember this particular story. My mother was a chain smoker. Newport 100 lights. She would smoke all the time. When my sister was young she had a long lasting cough. Because of it my mother took her to the local clinic. My sister was diagnosed with asthma and the very honest doctor told my mother that it was due to her smoking. I don't know the exact details of how that conversation went down or how my mother received it, but I do know that shortly there afterward my mother decided to quit smoking. And I'm not talking about quit smoking by weaning herself off slowly, smoking four cigarettes per day instead of the whole pack. I'm not talking about getting a nicotine patch or chewing a special kind of gum. No. I'm talking about crazy old school cold turkey quit smoking. She was not a nice person when she quit. Although yelling was her usual form of communication it did take a major increase in frequency and octave during this time. I remember as a kid not understanding why she was even *meaner* than before. It wasn't until I became an adult and put the pieces together that I recognized that her attitude shift was because she was in the midst of this physical battle trying to overcome her smoking addiction for the betterment of her child's health. Here's what I did know though, even as a child- When my mother decided to do something, she just did it! Regardless of how hard it was going to be, regardless of the struggle that was to follow, and regardless of the pain- she was going to do it.

Similarly, when she decided that she wanted to get her GED she went down to the office, signed up for the classes, and studied like it was nobody's business. Not only did she test before everyone else in her entire group but she blew the test away. She made a decision, she followed through, and she made it happen. When she decided to move us to Massachusetts, she made a decision, she followed through and she made it happen. When she decided to quit smoking she made a decision, she followed through, and she made it happen.

As an adult I realize that what drove her was the why. The why is the purpose behind the goal. She had to find and tap into a really strong reason to want something better. And once she found- that thing was as good as done! I've learned this, along with many other wonderful lessons, from my mother. I tell you this because I know that sometimes when we make a decision what follows is an uphill battle. When we tap into the purpose behind the goal and determine that is the most important reason to follow through, we will. When we tap into the purpose and make that our driving force, keep that at the forefront of our minds, and remind ourselves continuously then we can make it happen, we will. So, this leaves me needing to ask you: Why do you want to live a super sparkly everything life?

Make It Real.

I'm not just asking just to ask. I want you to take a moment and actually answer the following questions in your journal. Be as detailed as possible.

1. How would you define a super sparkly everything life for yourself?

2. Why do you want to live a super sparkly everything life?

3. What would that look like?

4. What would that feel like?

5. What do your relationships look and feel like?

6. How are you loving yourself on a daily basis?

7. How far away is your current life from that desired life?

Glitter Everywhere.

Here you are! You've finished the book! Congratulations! I am so excited for you! Even if you just read through the book without doing any of the exercises, at least you read it. That is a reason to celebrate. Take a moment to give yourself a high five, to a little dance or share a hug with someone.

Now it's time to make a decision. Do you want a better life? If the answer is yes then you have to decide where you want to start. You can select a chapter, go back to the **Make It Real** section, and get to work. I once heard someone say if you want great legs you have to do squats. No one else can do your squats for you. This is not that different. Instead of just getting great legs though, what you're designing and building for yourself is a great life. And you deserve it because it is your birthright.

If you're finally here at the conclusion chapter and along the way you have been pulling out your journal and you have been doing the exercises in the **Make It Real** sections- Congratulations!! Give yourself a high five! That is incredible and you deserve to celebrate yourself, all of your hard work, your diligence and your consistency. You are on your way to creating a super sparkly life for yourself! You have decided to take responsibility for your life. You are no longer a victim to the circumstances that are happening in your life or what happened in your past. You are victorious because you are a child of God. Taking responsibility gives you back control of your life. Welcome to being in charge of your own life. Welcome to making forward movement on your journey to live a more fulfilled, fun and love filled life. It's going to be spectacular!

As a child I grew up in poverty with a teenage mother and a father who was an abusive alcoholic and a drug addict. I was told directly and indirectly that I wouldn't be anything more than what was happening around me. I had low self-esteem, felt like I was never enough, that I didn't deserve good things, and that I wasn't worthy. My life was full of toxic relationships and was in constant struggle. I was taught because of my abuse to stay small, deny my truth, and hide my gifts. I lived as a victim, constantly blaming others for the outcome of my life. I was angry, negative and unable to forgive. I was frustrated and I was depressed. I was also physically broken and had to overcome physical hurdles in the midst of it all.

Through my relationship with God I am now a woman who has defied the statistics. I got myself some new rituals and standards and started to do the work to create a life that represented the love of God, a life that thanked Him for my gifts and talents, a life of purpose on purpose. I love myself! I know that I deserve abundance and all the wonderful things that life has to offer because I am a child of the most high. I am worthy of all good things. I have healthy relationships. I live a life of peace and joy because of consistent prayer and meditation. I live in my truth recognizing that my past is full of facts that no longer have power to be precursors to my future. I am positive and I forgive. I am happy and full of hope. I live a life of faith and miracles. Just about everyday, I wake up energized and every night I go to sleep feeling fulfilled. It's not perfect all the time but it's perfect for me. I am perfect in God's eyes and my own. At the same time, I accept that I am imperfect and still a work-in-progress, working everyday to be better than I was the day before. I use my gifts regularly and live in the light and sparkle that God has given me. Although it can be scary at times, I'm no longer afraid to share my stories because I know that they will help provide hope and freedom for others. I live a life of gratitude and of love.

In this book I've talked about the importance of putting God first, putting yourself second, controlling your thoughts to control your life, choosing happiness on a daily basis, living with an attitude of gratitude, protecting your temple and caring for your body with food and exercise, remembering that everyone including you, is on a journey, and the power that comes with taking responsibility for your life. You are your own hero. You get to wear the cape and save the day. You choice.

Okay. So now you have a list of things to do and steps to accomplish. Get started. Pick one. Any one. Action is necessary in order to use all of your knowledge to create positive change in your life. Write something. Share something. Volunteer. Start a group. Create something. Host a hangout. Do something! You know that vision that God put inside of you? Yes, that one. Well, it's time to take that from your mind and heart, and bring it into your reality. It's time to make it real! Now is the time for you to take the next step. On the beautiful journey to live in super sparkly everything life, there is always a next step. What that looks like, only you can decide.

My Prayer for You

I pray that you see this moment for what it is and acknowledge this moment, right now. I pray that you constantly acknowledge that life is full of beautiful things and that you see them with gratitude and love. I pray that you stand in gratitude and love when you forgive both yourself and others, and when you take responsibility for every area of your life. I pray that you always see yourself as the masterpiece that you are, the way God sees you. I pray that you love yourself unconditionally. I pray that you remember that you can start over every day, with every new rain and in between the rainy days. I pray that you remember to be patient with yourself and that you extend that same patience to others. I pray that you self care regularly and invest in your body, mind and spirit. I pray that you release toxic relationships and send them away with love because your new mandates demand more. I pray that your life is filled with amazing people who love and support you in word and in deed. I pray that you make healthy decisions for your life based on love. I pray that you create new mandates, new rituals and new standards that will bring your life to a higher level. I pray that you give yourself permission to make changes and to change your mind. I pray that you remember the journey, enjoying it and celebrating it along the way. I pray that you allow yourself to live in the abundance and fullness that God has promised. I pray that you find new levels and new ways to be the best version of yourself day in and day out. I pray that you consistently give yourself permission to live in all of your light, in all of your fullness and in all of your sparkle. You deserve it and there is no better place to be. I pray that your life from this moment forward is **Super Sparkly Everything!**

With love and gratitude, Maria Milagros

Chapter 14

EXTRAS AND REFERENCES

It's never too late to start over. If you weren't happy with yesterday, try something different today. Don't stay stuck. Do better. ~Alex Elle

In this chapter you will find the following:

A. Seven Quick Steps to Turn Around Your Day
B. Starting Affirmations
C. Becoming the Person You Want to Become Exercise
D. My 3 Life Mottos Explained with Affirmations
E. Scriptures for Each Chapter
F. Ways to Get More Super Sparkly Everything

****

A. *Seven Quick Steps to Turn Around Your Day*

We all have bad days. That is real because we are living and bad things happen. We get to choose whether we surrender the entire day to the one moment that forced us upside down. We usually look back and are bothered that we spent so much time worrying or upset about a situation that didn't deserve that much energy. In usual fashion, here are a few tips for a quick turn around. You deserve to take the time to do this when you're mad, sad, frustrated, disappointed etc. Use your energy to complete these steps and save your day. Or, use your energy to stay in that negative place. You choice.

1. Write a list of all of the things that you are currently grateful for. All. From the little things like the clothes on your body, to the important and useful things like running water, to the greatest things like every person that you love and who loves you. All.

2. Re-read that list.

3. Write a list of the things you need to do before the day ends, at least 3. This can include a work project, an errand, a household chore or hugging a loved one. Put it on the list and prioritize it.

4. Re-read your gratitude list while listening to your favorite upbeat and positive song.

5. Move. Dance. Walk. Get moving even for just a few minutes. Your physiology changes your psychology.

6. Take a moment to thank someone or send a quick note or email of gratitude to express your appreciation or love.

7. Re-read your list and realize that you have so much to be grateful for, a list of tasks that you are trusted

with and capable of accomplishing, you can move, and you have people to be grateful for.

You're welcome.

****

B. *Starting Affirmations*

As discussed early on in this book the importance and the power of words cannot be denied. Namely, the words that we speak over ourselves and over our lives. I recommend writing your own affirmations in the positive, in the present and in the first person. Here are 10 affirmation examples in the top 7 life categories to get you started.

Spiritual

1. The power of Jesus and the Holy Spirit live in me. This greatness that lives in me is able to overcome and bring prosperity to me and my life.
2. I am strong, courageous, creative, resourceful, intelligent and can handle anything life throws my way. God is with me everywhere I go.
3. This will turn out in my favor because I am called and I believe. All things will work together to bring what is good and pleasing into my life.
4. I am a child of the most high God. He is always for me and has plans to prosper and protect me. I stay focused on that reality for my life.
5. In prayer my heavenly Father hears me and because I put Him first, He will fulfill my needs and the desires of my heart.

6. I will do what I can in every situation to the best of my ability. I will depend on God because he will always help me and strengthen me.
7. I am loved by God. I am a child of God.
8. I love God and strive to understand His ways.
9. I have found favor in the eyes of God and man.
10. I am positive and confident, and operate under perfect faith.

Personal

1. I love myself unconditionally.
2. I deeply appreciate and accept myself.
3. I am patient with myself as I progress towards continual greatness.
4. I deserve the best that life has to offer.
5. I am confident and self-assured.
6. I do my best and my best is always enough.
7. I am grateful for where I am and where I am headed.
8. I am positive, present and productive.
9. I am a necessary and an important part of the divine plan.
10. I do and pursue what I love because I am capable and worthy.

Emotional/Mental

1. The struggles of today develop, within me, the strength for tomorrow. That strength will benefit every area of my life and help me inspire the lives of others.
2. I am free from any hindrance and able to raise above all circumstances.

3. My emotions are always under control because I know that God is in control.
4. I am willing to take the risks necessary to live my life openly and honestly.
5. I acknowledge my feelings as a necessary part of my healing process.
6. I fill my mind with positive, nurturing and healing thoughts.
7. I forgive myself for love and affection that I withheld from myself and others.
8. I forgive others for hurting me and release them with love.
9. I am a good person and deserve to be happy and healthy.
10. I approach each day with enthusiasm and sleep fulfilled, knowing that I was able to contribute to the world for the better.

Physical

1. I sleep peacefully through the night and wake up well rested and refreshed.
2. My body is whole, healthy and healed.
3. Every bone, muscle, fiber and bone of my body operates in accordance with its purpose, individually and united.
4. My body is an amazing machine capable of anything.
5. I fuel my body with the food, exercise, rest and conditions that it needs to maintain its health.
6. I have 20/20 vision.
7. I recognize my body's needs and I meet them.
8. I generate positive and vibrant energy and bring it everywhere I go.
9. I look and feel amazing in my skin and in my body.

10.   I love my body.

Intellectual

1.   I am a learner. I am capable of learning anything with time, discipline and consistency.
2.   I am open to new knowledge and information that will continuously better my life.
3.   I have an amazing memory and capacity of learning, connecting and making associations for my memory.
4.   I am a seeker of inspiration and creativity.
5.   I look for, seek out, and find creativity and knowledge.
6.   I am confident to implement and use my knowledge to benefit every area of my life.
7.   I use my knowledge to find solutions, recognize options, and choices. I make great decisions.
8.   I am successful in every arena of my life.
9.   I call positive, inspiring, motivating and uplifting friends, mentors and teachers into my life.
10.   I complete all projects, tasks and learning that benefit my life.

Relational

1.   I am blessed and a blessing to others.
2.   I am capable of sharing and accepting love.
3.   I am a loving, kind and patient _____.
       (mother, father, sister, brother, cousin, friend, etc.)
4.   I ask for what I need with truth and love.
5.   My presence impacts others for the better.
6.   I am articulate and able to express myself so that others understand me.
7.   I seek to understand others, remembering that they are on their own journey.

8.   I have amazing supportive relationships and I am the _____ (spouse, friend, employee, etc) that I will allow in my life.
9.   I invite only healthy, honest, loving and supportive relationships into my life.
10. I treat others from a place of gratitude and love in every situation and circumstance.

Financial

1.   I am deserving and worthy of monetary prosperity.
2.   I receive bonuses, raises, checks in the mail and am limitless in my finances.
3.   I give generously and reap generously.
4.   I do a wonderful work in a wonderful way. I give wonderful service for a wonderful pay.
5.   I live in financial freedom.
6.   I am a good steward with all that I am trusted with, including my finances.
7.   I am an irresistible magnet for all that is mine by divine right.
8.   I trust myself to manage money honestly and sensibly.
9.   I am able to have more money than I need.
10. I can make all the money I need doing a job I love.

****

C. '*Becoming the Person You Want to Become' Exercise*

Here are the steps for the exercise to figuring out what qualities you admire in others and would like to develop for yourself. It will help you figure out what to do while you are becoming the person you want to be.

1.Write down the names of all of the people that you look up to or admire, who have inspired you and so on. Leave some space under each name.

2. Under every person's name, write the words that describe why you look up to them. Are they funny, knowledgeable, charming, a good speaker? Write all of those things.

3. Look at that list of characteristics. Are there any of those qualities that you have? Yes, of course, circle those.
Are there any on the list that you wish you had? Highlight those or put a star next to them.

4. Separate the list into qualities that you already have and qualities you want to develop.

5. Write a separate list of the qualities, characteristics or skills that you want to develop or hone.

6. Look at your new list, pick one thing that you can start working on immediately to develop or hone.

7. Now, you have to actually have to find a book, seminar, class or program that will help you develop that quality, characteristic or skill.

Doing that will help you feel more confident about who you are and allows you to take responsibility for who you need to become to accomplish what you need to accomplish.

****

D. *My 3 Life Mottos Explained*

I have 3 life mottos. Every morning I repeat these three as part of my affirmations and every evening I check in with myself to see if I lived these out during my day. The three models are: 1. living my truth, 2. taking responsibility for my life, and 3. acting and responding from a place of love and gratitude towards God, myself, others, situations and events. I strongly urge you to discover what your 3 top mottos, your mandates are, and build from there. Allow me to take a moment here to break down what mine are and what they represent for me with affirmative declarations. You can use this as a template or a starting point to create your own.

I live in my truth.

- I love God and believe in His power in my life.
- I am a child of God and as such I am deserving and worthy of all the good that life has to offer.
- I love my body and treated it as such.
- I am a loving mother and make decisions accordingly.
- I was abused mentally, emotionally, sexually, and physically. Those are facts not my future.
- I am honest and work continuously to deliver honesty from a place of love.
- I'm working on myself. I am always in progress.
- I love myself, my body, my quirks, my ways, my mind, and my spirit. I love me. I love Maria.
- I am grateful and expectant.
- I am content with little and with much.
- I am broken and imperfect and that is okay.
- I am creative and energetic.
- I am intelligent.
- I am personable and outgoing.

- I enjoyed dancing, writing, painting, and being artistically creative.
- I make crazy facial expressions.
- I can be loud and I love to laugh.

I take responsibility for my life.

- I fuel my body with healthy, balanced, and nourishing food.
- I cook most of my meals.
- I exercise regularly to keep my body strong.
- I take time to affirm myself and meditate.
- I take time daily to do something that brings me joy.
- I am victorious over my past.
- I read my Bible, pray and spend time with God daily.
- I make time to care for my spine daily.
- I make time for my daughter on a daily basis.
- I make time for my relationships.
- I live in accordance with my means and budget accordingly.
- I called abundance into my life daily.
- I use my gifts to help others find their freedom.
- I take care of my body with rest, sleep, food, water, etc. when I'm not feeling well.
- I take time to learn and grow in areas that are important and interesting to me.
- I take responsibility, hold myself accountable, apologize, and forgive.
- I am the source of my happiness and tap into that every day.
- I consciously take control of my thoughts and thereby take control of my life.
- I exercise an attitude of gratitude daily.
- I work hard to be the best version of myself.
- My competition is me from yesterday.

I act and respond from a place of love and gratitude towards God, myself, others, situations and events.

- I am thankful in every situation. There's always a lesson to be learned or something good to take away.
- I ask "What's good about this?"
- I treat others with love, remembering that they are also on their own journey.
- I remember that there is/was a purpose, reason and season for every relationship.
- I am patient with myself and with others.
- I'm grateful and loving while in a relationship and grateful when it is over.
- I am appreciative of the lessons that every relationship teaches me.
- I look to events in my life as opportunities to make a positive impact. I show up as myself and in my truth with the intent to spread love and encourage others to find their freedom.
- I tell people why I love and am thankful for them.
- I love myself. I make decisions accordingly.
- I remember that hurt people hurt people. I love them anyways. I don't take it personal.
- I love toxic people from a distance. Self-love does not allow them into my life. I surrender them to God and pray for them often.
- I help others when and where I can.
- I take time to recharge and refuel so that I can continue to do the work that God has called me to do.
- I am blessed to be a blessing.

****

E. *My Top Seven Related Scriptures per Chapter*

Chapter 1: Allow Me To Clarify

1. **John 8:32-** Then you will know the truth, and the truth will set you free.
2. **Philippians 4:19-** And my God will supply all your needs according to His riches in glory in Christ Jesus.
3. **Joshua 1:9-** Have I not commanded you? Be strong and courageous. Do not be frightened, and do not be dismayed, for the Lord your God is with you wherever you go.
4. **Romans 8:28-** God has promised that all things work together for good to those who love and serve Him faithfully.
5. **Matthew 5:14-16-** You are the light of the world. A city set on a hill cannot be hidden; nor does anyone light a lamp and put it under a basket, but on the lamp stand, and it gives light to all who are in the house. "Let your light shine before men in such a way that they may see your good works, and glorify your Father who is in heaven."
6. **John 10:10-** Jesus came that we may have life and have it abundantly.
7. **Galatians 3:26-** For we are all children of God through faith in Christ Jesus.

****

Chapter 2: Time To Make a Decision

1. **Proverbs 16:1-3-** The plans of the heart belong to man, but the answer of the tongue is from the Lord. All the ways of a man are pure in his own eyes, but the Lord weighs the spirit. Commit your work to the Lord, and

your plans will be established. The Lord has made everything for its purpose, even the wicked for the day of trouble. Everyone who is arrogant in heart is an abomination to the Lord; be assured, he will not go unpunished.

2. **Psalm 25:4-** Make me to know your ways, O Lord; teach me your paths.
3. **Proverbs 12:15-** The way of a fool is right in his own eyes, but a wise man listens to advice.
4. **Proverbs 18:15-** An intelligent heart acquires knowledge, and the ear of the wise seeks knowledge.
5. **Proverbs 4:5-** Get wisdom; get insight; do not forget, and do not turn away from the words of my mouth.
6. **James 1:22-** But be doers of the word, and not hearers only, deceiving yourselves.
7. **Proverbs 27:17-** Iron sharpens iron, and one man sharpens another.

****

Chapter 3: The Why

1. **Proverbs 16:4-** The Lord has made everything for its purpose.
2. **1 Corinthians 10:31-** So, whether you eat or drink, or whatever you do, do all to the glory of God.
3. **Proverbs 16:9-** The heart of man plans his way, but the Lord establishes his steps.
4. **Jeremiah 1:4-5-** Now the word of the Lord came to me, saying, "Before I formed you in the womb I knew you, and before you were born I consecrated you; I appointed you a prophet to the nations."
5. **Proverbs 19:21-** Many are the plans in the mind of a man, but it is the purpose of the Lord that will stand.

6. **Romans 8:31-39-** For I am convinced that neither death nor life, neither angels nor demons, neither present nor future, nor any powers, neither height nor depth, nor anything else in all creation, will be able to separate us from the love of God.
7. **Exodus 18:14-27-** Moses father in law said to him, "What you are doing is no good. You and these people who come to you will only wear yourselves out. The work is too heavy for you; you cannot handle it alone."

****

Chapter 4: Fresh Start

1. **Romans 2:11-** God has no favorites.
2. **Genesis 11:6-** The Lord said, "If as one people speaking the same language they have begun to do this, then nothing they plan to do will be impossible for them.
3. **2 Peter 3:9-** The Lord is not slow in keeping his promise, as some understand slowness. Instead he is patient with you, not wanting anyone to perish, but everyone to come to repentance.
4. **Hebrews 6:19-** We have this hope as an anchor for the soul, firm and secure. It enters the inner sanctuary behind the curtain
5. **Hebrews 13:8-** Jesus Christ is the same yesterday and today and forever.
6. **2 Corinthians 4:16-18-** Therefore we do not lose heart. Though outwardly we are wasting away, yet inwardly we are being renewed day by day. For our light and momentary troubles are achieving for us an eternal glory that far outweighs them all. So we fix our eyes not on what is seen, but on what is unseen, since what is seen is temporary, but what is unseen is eternal.

7. **Psalm 103:2-5-** Praise the LORD, my soul, and forget not all his benefits— who forgives all your sins and heals all your diseases, who redeems your life from the pit and crowns you with love and compassion, who satisfies your desires with good things so that your youth is renewed like the eagle's.

****

Chapter 5: Lucky Number 7

1. **Romans 8:1-** There is therefore no condemnation to them which are in Christ, who walk not after the flesh, but after the Spirit
2. **Mark 12:31-** The second is this: "Love your neighbor as yourself. There is no commandment greater than these."
3. **Psalm 139:14-** I praise you because I am fearfully and wonderfully made; your works are wonderful, I know that full well.
4. **2 Corinthians 9:8-** And God will generously provide all you need. Then you will always have everything you need and plenty left over to share with others.
5. **Genesis 50:20-** You intended to harm me, but God intended it for good to accomplish what is now being done, the saving of many lives.
6. **Proverbs 23:7-** For as he thinks within himself, so he is.
7. **Ephesians 4:26-** Be angry without sinning. Don't go to bed angry. Bonus: Psalm 16:11 ESV- You make known to me the path of life; in your presence there is fullness of joy; at your right hand are pleasures forevermore.

****

Chapter 6: Principle 1- Put God First

1. **Matthew 6:33-** But seek first the kingdom of God and his righteousness, and all these things will be added to you.
2. **Hebrews 11:6-** And without faith it is impossible to please him, for whoever would draw near to God must believe that he exists and that he rewards those who seek him.
3. **Proverbs 3:6-** In all your ways acknowledge him, and he will make straight your paths.
4. **James 1:17-** Every good gift and every perfect gift is from above, coming down from the Father of lights with whom there is no variation or shadow due to change.
5. **John 3:16-** For God so loved the world, that he gave his only Son, that whoever believes in him should not perish but have eternal life.
6. **Joshua 1:8-** This Book of the Law shall not depart from your mouth, but you shall meditate on it day and night, so that you may be careful to do according to all that is written in it. For then you will make your way prosperous, and then you will have good success.
7. **Micah 7:18-** Who is a God like you, pardoning iniquity and passing over transgression for the remnant of his inheritance?....he delights in steadfast love.

****

Chapter 7: Principle 2- Love Yourself

1. **1 Corinthians 13:4-8-** Love is patient, love is kind. It does not envy, it does not boast, it is not proud. It does not dishonor others, it is not self-seeking, it is not easily

angered, it keeps no record of wrongs. Love does not delight in evil but rejoices with the truth. It always protects, always trusts, always hopes, always perseveres. Love never fails.

2. **1 Corinthians 13:10-13-** ...but when completeness comes, what is in part disappears. When I was a child, I talked like a child, I thought like a child, I reasoned like a child. When I became a woman, I put the ways of childhood behind me. For now we see only a reflection as in a mirror; then we shall see face to face. Now I know in part; then I shall know fully, even as I am fully known. And now these three remain: faith, hope and love. But the greatest of these is love.

3. **2 Peter 1:3-** His divine power (love) has given us everything we need for a godly life through our knowledge of Him who called us by His own glory and goodness.

4. **2 Corinthians 1:20-** For no matter how many promises God has made, they are "YES" in Christ, and so through him the "AMEN" is spoken by us to the glory of God.

5. **Luke 7:48-** Then Jesus said to her, "Your sins are forgiven."

6. **Mark 6:31-** Come with me by yourselves to a quiet place and get some rest. So they went away by themselves in a boat to a solitary place.

7. **Ephesians 2:10-** For YOU are God's masterpiece! He has created YOU anew in Christ Jesus, so YOU can do good things He planned for YOU long ago.

****

Chapter 8: Principle 3- Control Your Thoughts

1. **Proverbs 23:7-** Or for as he thinks within himself, so he is.
2. **Romans 12:2-** Do not be conformed to this world, but be transformed by the renewal of your mind, that by testing you may discern what is the will of God, what is good and acceptable and perfect.
3. **Proverbs 3:5-6-** Trust in the Lord with all your heart and do not rely on your own understanding. Acknowledge Him in all your ways and he will make your paths straight.
4. **Philippians 4:8-** Finally, brothers, whatever is true, whatever is honorable, whatever is just, whatever is pure, whatever is lovely, whatever is commendable, if there is any excellence, if there is anything worthy of praise, think about and focus on these things.
5. **Romans 8:1-** There is therefore now no condemnation for those who are in Christ Jesus.
6. **Hebrews 4:12-** For the word of God is living and active, sharper than any two-edged sword, piercing to the division of soul and of spirit, of joints and of marrow, and discerning the thoughts and intentions of the heart.
7. **2 Timothy 1:7-** For God gave us a spirit not of fear but of power and love and self-control.

****

Chapter 9: Principle 4- Protect Your Temple.

1. **3 John 1:2-** Beloved, I pray that all may go well with you and that you may be in good health, as it goes well with your soul.

2. **1 Corinthians 6:19-20-** Or do you not know that your body is a temple of the Holy Spirit within you, whom you have from God? You are not your own, for you were bought with a price. So glorify God in your body.
3. **1 Corinthians 10:31-** So, whether you eat or drink, or whatever you do, do all to the glory of God.
4. **1 Corinthians 6:20-** For you were bought with a price. So glorify God in your body.
5. **Colossians 3:17-** And whatever you do, in word or deed, do everything in the name of the Lord Jesus, giving thanks to God the Father through him.
6. **1 Proverbs 31:17-** She sets about her work vigorously; her arms are strong for her tasks.
7. **1 Timothy 4:8-** For while bodily training is of some value, godliness is of value in every way, as it holds promise for the present life and also for the life to come.

****

Chapter 10: Principle 5- Life is a Journey.

1. **1 John 4:4-** You, dear children, are from God and have overcome them (problems, enemies, struggles), because the one who is in you (Jesus and the Holy Spirit) is greater than the one that is in the world.
2. **Joshua 1:9-** Have I not commanded you? Be strong and courageous. Do not be afraid; do not be discouraged, for the Lord your God will be with you wherever you go.
3. **1 Peter 1:18-21-** Your life is a journey you must travel with a deep consciousness of God. It cost God plenty to get you out of that dead-end, empty-headed life you grew up in. He paid with Christ's sacred blood, you know. He died like an unblemished, sacrificial lamb.

And this was no afterthought. Even though it has only lately—at the end of the ages—become public knowledge, God always knew he was going to do this for you. It's because of this sacrificed Messiah, whom God then raised from the dead and glorified, that you trust God, that you know you have a future in God.

4. **Romans 8:18-** I consider that our present sufferings are not worth comparing with the glory that will be revealed in us.

5. **Isaiah 41:10-** So do not fear, for I am with you; do not be dismayed, for I am your God. I will strengthen you and help you; I will uphold you with my righteous right hand.

6. **Jeremiah 29:11-**"For I know the plans I have for you," declares the Lord, "plans to prosper you and protect you, plans to give you hope and a future."

7. **1 John 5:14-** This is the confidence we have in approaching God: that if we ask anything according to His will, He hears us.

****

Chapter 11: Principle 6- Who You With?

1. **1 Corinthians 15:33-** Do not be deceived: "Bad company ruins good morals."

2. **Genesis 2:18-** Then the Lord God said, "It is not good that the man should be alone; I will make him a helper fit for him."

3. **Ecclesiastes 4:9-12-** Two are better than one, because they have a good reward for their toil. For if they fall, one will lift up his fellow. But woe to him who is alone when he falls and has not another to lift him up! Again, if two lay together, they keep warm, but how can one keep warm alone? And though a man might prevail

against one who is alone, two will withstand him—a threefold cord is not quickly broken.

4. **Amos 3:3-** "Do two walk together, unless they have agreed to meet?"
5. **Romans 12:17-** Repay no one evil for evil, but give thought to do what is honorable in the sight of all.
6. **Proverbs 13:20-** Whoever walks with the wise becomes wise, but the companion of fools will suffer harm.
7. **1 Thessalonians 5:11-** Therefore encourage one another and build one another up, just as you are doing.

****

Chapter 12: Principle 7- You're The Hero

1. **Ezra 10:4 -**Arise, for it is your task, and we are with you; be strong and do it.
2. **Exodus 20:12-** Honor your father and your mother, that your days may be long in the land that the Lord your God is giving you.
3. **Ephesians 4:32-** Be kind to one another, tenderhearted, forgiving one another, as God in Christ forgave you.
4. **Mark 11:25-**And whenever you stand praying, forgive, if you have anything against anyone, so that your Father also who is in heaven may forgive you your trespasses.
5. **Matthew 11:28 -**Come to me, all who labor and are heavy laden, and I will give you rest.
6. **2 Corinthians 5:17-** Therefore, if anyone is in Christ, he is a new creation. The old has passed away; behold, the new has come.
7. **Proverbs 16:3-** Commit to the Lord whatever you do, and he will establish your plans.

****

Chapter 13: And In Conclusion

1. **1 Chronicles 16:11-** Look to the LORD and his strength; seek his face always.
2. **James 1: 2-8 -** Consider it all joy, my brethren, when you encounter various trials, knowing that the testing of your faith produces endurance. And let endurance have its perfect result, so that you may be perfect and complete, lacking in nothing. But if any of you lacks wisdom, let him ask of God, who gives to all generously and without reproach, and it will be given to him. But he must ask in faith without any doubting, for the one who doubts is like the surf of the sea, driven and tossed by the wind. For that man ought not to expect that he will receive anything from the Lord, being a double-minded man, unstable in all his ways.
3. **1 Corinthians 13:11-** When I was a child, I spoke like a child, I thought like a child, I reasoned like a child. When I became a man, I gave up childish ways.
4. **Galatians 6:5-** For each will have to bear his own load.
5. **Colossians 3:23-** Whatever you do, work heartily, as for the Lord and not for men.
6. **Psalm 37:4-** Take delight in the LORD, and he will give you the desires of your heart.
7. **2 Corinthians 9:6-** The point is this: whoever sows sparingly will also reap sparingly, and whoever sows bountifully will also reap bountifully.

****

Chapter 14: Extras and References

1. **Proverbs 16:16-** How much better to get wisdom than gold! To get understanding is to be chosen rather than silver.

2. **Proverbs 4:13 -** Keep hold of instruction; do not let go; guard her, for she is your life.
3. **Proverbs 18:15-** An intelligent heart acquires knowledge, and the ear of the wise seeks knowledge.
4. **2 Timothy 3:16-** All Scripture is breathed out by God and profitable for teaching, for reproof, for correction, and for training in righteousness.
5. **Proverbs 1:7-** The fear of the Lord is the beginning of knowledge; fools despise wisdom and instruction.
6. **Proverbs 1:5-** Let the wise hear and increase in learning, and the one who understands obtain guidance.
7. **James 1:5-** If any of you lacks wisdom, let him ask God, who gives generously to all without reproach, and it will be given him.

"You are altogether beautiful, my darling, there is NO flaw in you."
Song of Solomon 4:7

****

F. *More Super Sparkly Everything*

- Share your experience with this book or your testimony by emailing me at supersparklyeverything@gmail.com

- Sign up for my FREE monthly newsletter and weekly videos at www.mariamilagros.net

- Subscribe to my YouTube page by finding MariaMila Vazquez

- Follow me on Facebook at https://www.facebook.com/MariaMilagros777

- Follow me on Instagram @MariaMilaVazquez

- Sign up to take one of my online courses at https://maria-milagros-freedom-academy.teachable.com

- Learn more about my Life Coaching services at www.mariamilagros.net

- Learn more about my Mentoring services at www.mariamilagros.net

THANK YOU

First and foremost I must give all praise and glory to my Heavenly Father. It is the love that He shows me that allows me to do what I am called to do. There are so many people that have helped me along the way, both directly and inadvertently. It would probably take a whole new chapter to list everyone so here is the shortest version of that list.

Naima Cecilia, when I told you I was starting to write my book, you asked me everyday how it was going and consistently told me that I was doing a good job. You are the reason that I knew that I had to write this book, in order to share my story, to help others, and to show you that if you set your mind to it, you can accomplish your goals. I learn something new from you everyday, your antics make me laugh, you remind me to stay present, and you keep me grounded while encouraging me to soar. You make me want to be the best version of myself day in and day out so that I can be the best mother for you. I carry your heart in my heart. I love you mucho y siempre!

Sophia Richardson, sistergurl. I appreciate and love you so much! You have been by my side and have always been honest with me. You push me when I need the push, listen when I need an ear and have always been a source of love and support, even when I come up with some crazy ideas. Thank you!

Angela Morales, thank you for your openness, your kind spirit, your love and friendship. Thank you for offering to edit this book. This book wouldn't have been complete without your help. I appreciate you on so many levels and for so many reasons. I love you.

Kimatra Maxwell, thank you for showing up at the perfect time in my life and for always being honest with me. Thank you for always accepting all of my crazy and embracing it without judgement. My life is better because you are in it and you are a constant inspiration to me. I love you.

Laura Wisler, thank you for being who you are. Thank you for your constant support and for being my sounding board for everything. Thank you for your consistent caring and for reminding me to always push myself, to learn and to grow. Thank you for inspiring me every time we talk. I love you.

Trever Zarycki, for being one of my best friends, for making me laugh, and for loving me in a way that I've never known before you. Knowing you has been a gift and I appreciate and love you more than you know.

Marta Albizu, because I know that you have always done the best you could with what you knew how. I appreciate you, all of the lessons I've learned from you, and your heart. Whether you realize it or not, you have taught me how to fight for what I deserve, how to follow through and how to move on. With love, thank you.

An extra special thank you to the following people for their continued positivity, love and support: Julio Alvarez, Raquel Andrews, Natonia Trammell, Magdiel DeLeon, Jason Morales, Michael Maxwell, all of my fantastic nieces and nephews, Brian Sullivan, Jerry Albizu, Andrea Ramos, Myriah Zwicker, Meloney Cole, LaKesha Gunn, and Jackie Jennings.

Thank you to the following people for being a source of assistance, encouragement and/or inspiration over the years: Ms. Rey, Dr. James Cormier, MaryAnn Macri, Carey Doucette, Danielle Drapeau, Miriam Cronin, Terry Beck, Emy and Emily Vazquez, Dalphane Albizu, Deborah Fnine, Patty Sparks, Tricia May, Donald Flagg, Sabrina Walker, Bob Donahue, Liz Gonzalez, Mark Goguen, Richard Mascherelli, and my incredible dance students.

ABOUT THE AUTHOR

Maria Milagros is first and foremost a child of the Most High God. She is a mother to an amazing and brilliant little girl. She enjoys sharing her life lessons and knowledge through motivational talks, workshops, classes, videos, dance, spoken word, or poetry. She uses encouragement, education and love to empower others to live the Super Sparkly Everything kind of life. Her goal is to help others find spiritual, emotional and mental, health, and financial freedom.

When she is not creating or choreographing, playing with her daughter, or spending time with her family, you can find her working out, reading, or dancing in a public place. She strives to live a free, fulfilled and joy-filled life regardless of her past or her life's circumstances. She knows that a relationship to God and personal responsibility changed every area of her life for the better. She is not an exception to the rule. If she can do it, then you can too!

Maria Milagros Vazquez

.

Made in the USA
Middletown, DE
11 March 2023

26471103R00118